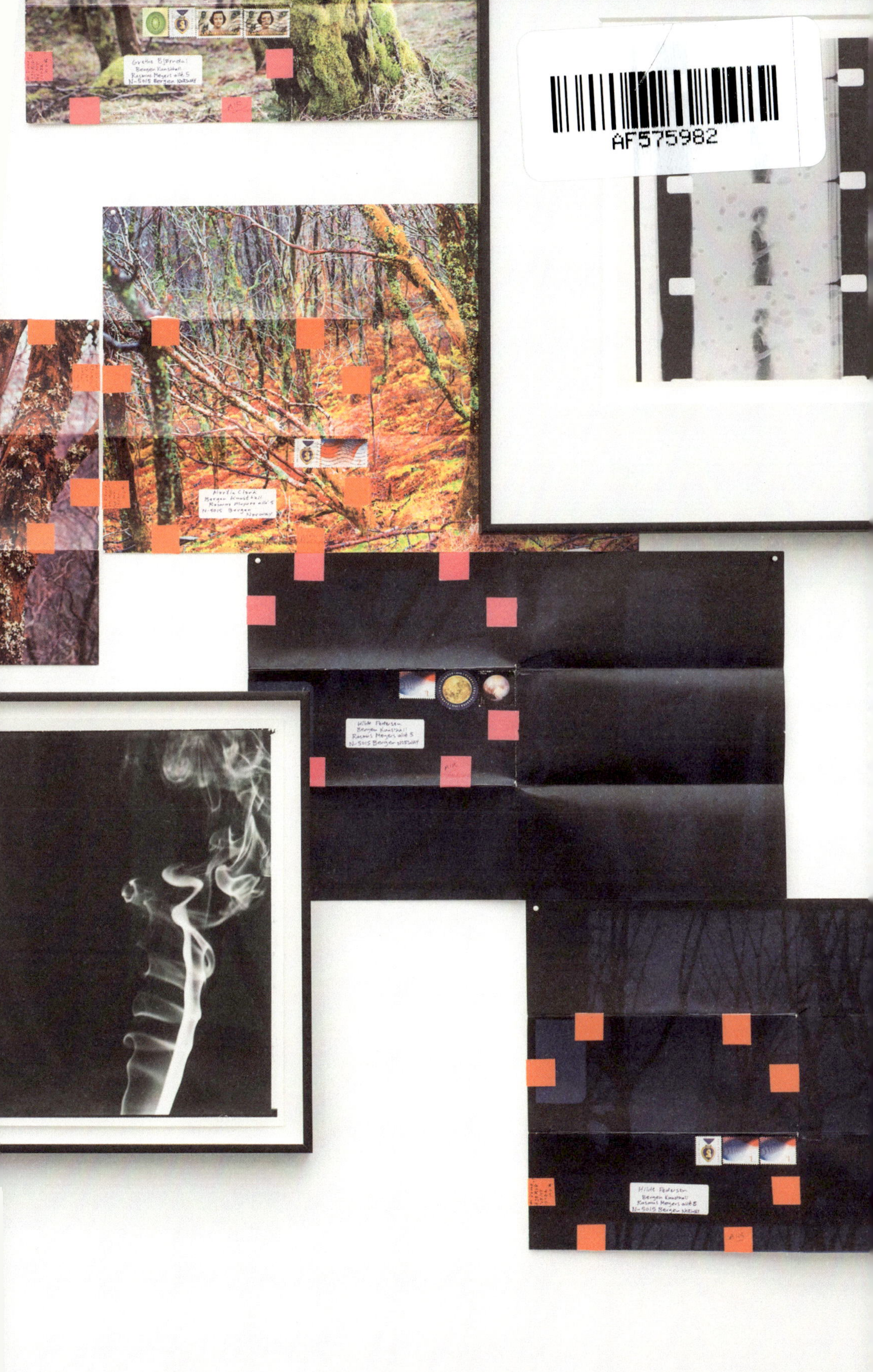
AF575982

LES GODDESSES

Moyra Davey

HEMLOCK FOREST

WITH A TEXT BY

Aveek Sen

Bergen Kunsthall
Dancing Foxes Press, Brooklyn

CONTENTS

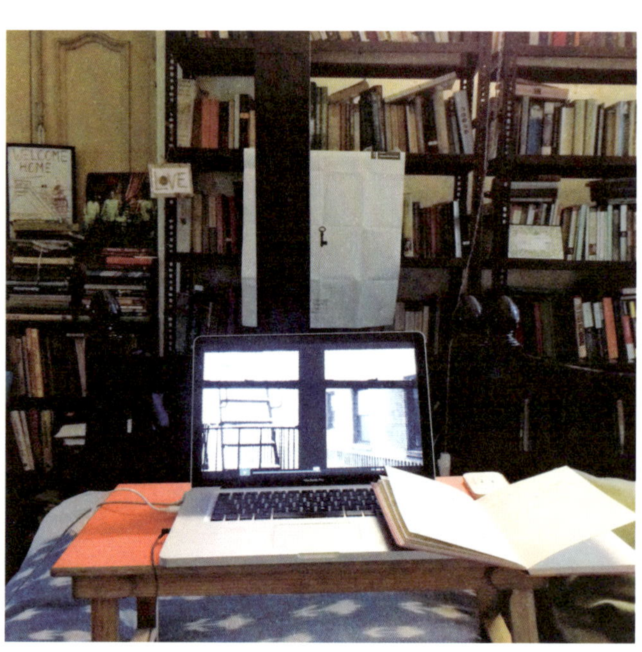
WELCOME
HOME
LOVE

AVEEK SEN

Low-Hanging Fruit

Imogen: Think that you are upon a rock, and now
Throw me again. [*Embracing him*]
Posthumus: Hang there like fruit, my soul,
Till the tree die!
Cymbeline: How now, my flesh? My child?
What, mak'st thou me a dullard in this act?
Wilt thou not speak to me?
—William Shakespeare, *Cymbeline*, act 5, scene 5, lines 262-66

I

The window and the bed: two frames, each a grid; two planes perpendicular to each other but keeping each other in sight. Together they form the geometry of my viewing, inside of which the filmmaker, writer, reader, and speaker moves. They are held, in turn, on the screen of my laptop, placed on my bed. I look up from time to time in order to look out of two windows in front of me. As I view the films over and over again, I make notes. My open notebook is the other plane, the third, with its counterpart in the many books and pages in the films I am watching—books, notes, and screens from which the artist reads.

As I watch the films and make notes, an anxiety builds in me. What if my viewing of the films and then my thinking and writing about them never manage to get beyond this three-planed geometry, beyond "the is-ness of what is"?[1] What if, caught within my repeated viewing of the films, I end up rehearsing their words and actions, copying into my notes what the filmmaker reads out incessantly? She reads, she makes notes, she writes, she films what she reads and writes, she makes films in which she reads out what she writes; I write in my notes what she reads out about what she has read, I read up on what she has read. What if I am trapped in this cycle, this infinite regress, of reading, writing, filming, and making notes? Does this cycle encircle or exclude the Real? And how do I get to that Real—her Real, my Real, and the interface of our two Reals? Do I get to it by stepping out of this circle of reading-writing-filming-viewing-writing-and-reading or by looking into it and then out through it? How do I produce a critical and responsive metalanguage that captures the Real of my viewing? How do I say something *about* the films, beyond simply viewing them, describing them, transcribing them, and re-presenting them in writing? The activity of making notes is like a "mothering," the filmmaker writes, quoting from a book I too possess, read from time to time, and write in: "I return to *notatio* as to a mother who protects me."[2] "Prisons I found rather motherly," she writes in another book, quoting someone else.[3] Notes, mothers, and prisons begin to come together in my head. How do I escape? How do I let my writing out?

I move, look up, from bed to window—her window. That's the escape. (The two meanings of *looking up* collide: "looking up" as an optical and postural distraction from reading and writing, and the act of "looking up" a reference—an elaboration, as well as an intensification, of reading.) I see the New York skyline. I see the water towers on the terraces. But before I mark these, I keep noticing across the films the leitmotif of knotted curtains, which let in the light and the view, yet tie something tightly in. I link them with a word, a quality, from one of the films: tightfisted, tightfistedness. They are like fists, holding on to something (a Cartier-Bresson photograph from *Europeans* fleetingly comes to mind). The light that comes through allows the dust to be seen as it is blown off the tops of books. They make me think of how generosity and ungenerosity, openness and opacity, are often inseparable in the making of art and the writing of texts: what is given (given out, given away, given up) and what is not (not given in to, what is resisted and withheld). *Reticence, retreat*: keywords in the films. They make me think of the voice of the films, relentlessly confessional yet wary, reserved, and deadpan—giving and ungiving at the same time, unfeelingly talking about unspeakable feelings.

The knotted curtains lead, in my memory and notes, to another action: how she takes off her bra without taking off her T-shirt. (I have another friend who does this too, skillfully, even during sit-down dinners, without anyone noticing. She too is a reader, writer, and talker.) Again, in that particular piece of action, release and concealment come together with an almost shocking dexterity; she is simultaneously thrifty and prodigal. I think of Mary Wollstonecraft opening her bosom to the embrace of nature. I think of her infected breast milk being sucked out by puppies. The filmmaker takes off her clothes but puts the bra back on, keeping it on in her nakedness on the bed, as she eats marshmallows generously dusted with powdered sugar and as the dog jumps up on the bed with her. I regress again toward the prison of description, to the bed. Go back to the window. Look up.

New York water towers. I think of Bernd and Hilla Becher and a photo history of typology and objectivity that the artist both brings into and keeps out of her films. My mind moves between New York and Paris with the films. Of what, or whom, does this journey remind me? My heart is racing now with the thrill of escape. I go to my shelves and take out a book I bought during my first, and only, visit to New York: *He Disappeared into Complete Silence*, a suite of nine engravings paired with little stories by Louise Bourgeois. Plate 9—with three mysteriously human tower-like structures out of which L. B. had made her *Personages*—came with this story:

> Once there was the mother of a son. She loved him with a complete devotion.
> And she protected him because she knew how sad and wicked this world is.
> He was of a quiet nature and rather intelligent but he was not interested in being loved or protected because he was interested in something else.
> Consequently at an early age he slammed the door and never came back.
> Later on she died but he did not know it.[4]

I have escaped. But it is an escape *into* the circle, perhaps even to the heart of it. I tell myself that I have been watching a filmmaker who has made books: I have just finished reading one on motherhood—breathlessly, often painfully, mostly in bed. It strikes me that it is called *Mother Reader*.

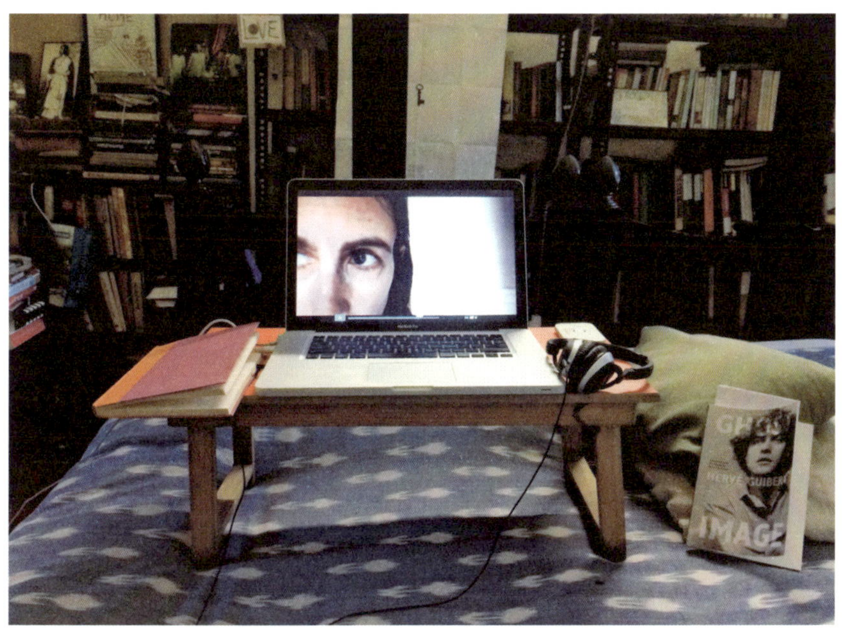
LOVE
IMAGE

II

Hemlock Forest and *Les Goddesses*, together and individually, seem to move restlessly between two unresolved anxieties: the fear of low-hanging fruit and the fear of the opposite of low-hanging fruit; between risking what is too easy and risking what is too difficult; between obtaining something too effortlessly and losing something through too much effort; between immediate access and denial of access. The metaphor of low-hanging fruit leads naturally, for me, to the oppressive sensibleness and comfort of William Godwin's advice to Mary that a "disappointed woman should try to construct happiness 'out of a set of materials *within [her] reach*.'"[5] What keeps these two anxieties distinct is the labor of reading, writing, thinking, connecting, of having to "make, make, make," and, I would risk adding (my own opposite of low-hanging fruit), of having been mothered and of being a mother. That last, for me, is the "raw and intractable" subject that dares not speak its name, which both eludes and confronts the artist, the mother-reader, as the immense void of apparent subjectlessness.

This void makes itself palpable to me in two ways: First, as I listen to the films closely, there is the primary speaking voice of the filmmaker and storyteller. But there is also the faint and fleeting pre-echo of another ghost voice. Between these two voices is a gap that is both auditory and temporal and across which the time-based medium of film barely manages to keep up with its subject as it tries to reach the viewer-listener. This phenomenon intrigues me, and I wonder how it can be explained technologically, until I read about the prerecorded audio prompt at the end of *Les Goddesses*. And because I still don't understand the technology fully—nor do I want to—this purely acoustic feature has become linked, in my experience of the films, to something essential and intangible, only just graspable, in them.

Second, this break in the acoustic voice of the films corresponds, for me, to a movement from one grammatical voice to another in the progression from *Les Goddesses* to *Hemlock Forest.* I hear this as a movement from the first person, what an astute commentator has described as the desperation of the personal voice, to the second and third persons—from the *I* in *Les Goddesses* to the *you* and the *she* (or a series of initials), but most vitally the *you,* in *Hemlock Forest.*[6] (Strictly speaking, it is a movement that happens within each film, rather than in a historical progression from the earlier to the later film. But I do hear it as an evolution in the artist's voice as well.) It is also a movement from one kind of risk, that of the first person, to another—dare I say, greater, though less obvious—risk: that of the second person, of addressing another person, who is both the addressee and the subject, or both the object and the subject, of the film. The latter is a risk that gets associated with the immorality or amorality of eavesdropping and image theft, conscious transgressions licensed by art.

It is not a coincidence that *Hemlock Forest* begins with unanswered letters from a worried mother to a self-absorbed daughter, who then reads these letters out in her own film instead of responding to them, thereby answering them and not answering them at the same time. And it is this epistolary voice—the mother writing to the daughter, inverted in the scenario of a mother addressing and filming her son (a son who prefers to watch planes flying in and out of airports to looking at art in museums)—that *Hemlock Forest* poses as the kind of risk that

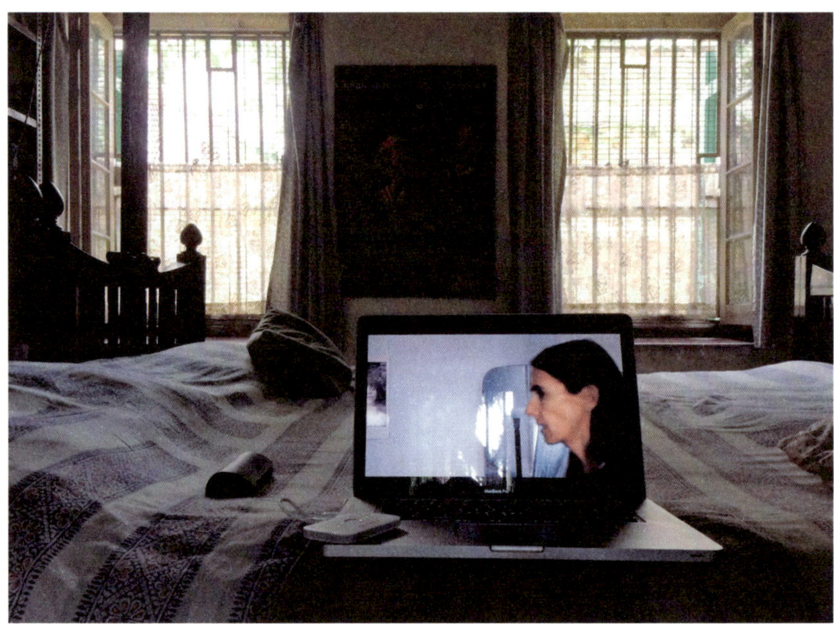

is opposite that of low-hanging fruit. There is in this risk another kind of desperation altogether, a desperation nevertheless transformed into value by art. It is far more daunting than the unscripted vérité of street or subway photography. It raises the question of a different kind of permission (and permissiveness) altogether. And between the two films, the unanswered letter (together with the absent, unaware, silent, or possibly indifferent addressee, the risk of the *you* as opposed to the abjection of *yours truly*) is associated not only with the mother-and-child pair but also with the lover-and-beloved pair, so that abandonment (achieved, imagined, or apprehended) becomes associated with both sets of relationships, the maternal as well as the sexual.

III

I find myself making my own montage, using three fragments of writing taken from the films. "To do without people is for photography the most impossible of renunciations."[7] *Les Goddesses* moves from this sentence by Walter Benjamin to the possibility of abandonment and then of retreat. Cut to Hannah Arendt writing of Isak Dinesen: "The reward of storytelling is to be able to let go."[8] One might move, then, from abandonment and retreat—which is to look at absence, as it were, from opposite ends of the stick—to an image that "holds" these opposites together in something like an oxymoron wrested from the language of religion that fuses piety and pity: "But now the boy is suddenly a man with one foot out the door and plays his cards close to his chest. He relaxed and opened up once over a bottle of champagne; he sat and talked for an hour, and I could see the tension drain from his face. Then something a bit more innocent happened: he put his head in my lap like a living

Pietà. He was slightly high. I'd been dying to hold him in my arms and squeeze his flesh like the chubby baby he'd once been. I said, 'You're a nice guy to let me hold you like this.'"[9] It is an image that the artist, in what she calls her circumspection, permits herself only in her writing, without seeking—or risking—its visual realization on film.

Calcutta, September 11, 2016

1. Moyra Davey, *Fifty Minutes* (2006, video, sound, 50 min.), quoting from Vivian Gornick, "Reading in an Age of Uncertainty," *Los Angeles Times*, December 30, 2001.
2. Moyra Davey, "Notes on Photography and Accident," in *Long Life Cool White: Photographs and Essays by Moyra Davey* (Cambridge, MA: MIT Press; New Haven, CT: Yale University Press, 2008), 87, quoting her own translation of Roland Barthes, *La Préparation du roman I et II: Cours et séminaires au Collège de France, 1978–1980*, Paris: Seuil/Sonopress, 2003, CD.
3. Moyra Davey, *Burn the Diaries* (Brooklyn, NY: Dancing Foxes Press; Vienna: Museum moderner Kunst Stiftung Ludwig Wien; Philadelphia: Institute of Contemporary Art, 2014), 21, quoting from Jean Genet, *Prisoner of Love*, trans. Barbara Bray (New York: New York Review of Books, 2003).
4. Louise Bourgeois, *He Disappeared into Complete Silence* (New York: Gemor Press, 1947), pl. 9.
5. Lyndall Gordon, quoting William Godwin, in Lyndall Gordon, *Vindication: A Life of Mary Wollstonecraft* (New York: Harper Perennial, 2005), 515. My italics.
6. Iman Issa, "The Artists' Artists," *Artforum* 51, no. 4 (December 2012): 120.
7. Moyra Davey, *Les Goddesses* (2011, HD video, color, sound, 61 min.), quoting from Walter Benjamin, "Little History of Photography," in *Selected Writings*, vol. 2, ed. Michael W. Jennings, Howard Eiland, and Gary Smith, trans. Rodney Livingstone and others (Cambridge, MA: Belknapp Press, 1999).
8. Davey, *Les Goddesses*, quoting from Hannah Arendt, "Isak Dinesen: 1885–1963," in *Men in Dark Times* (New York: Harcourt, 1955).
9. Davey, *Hemlock Forest*.

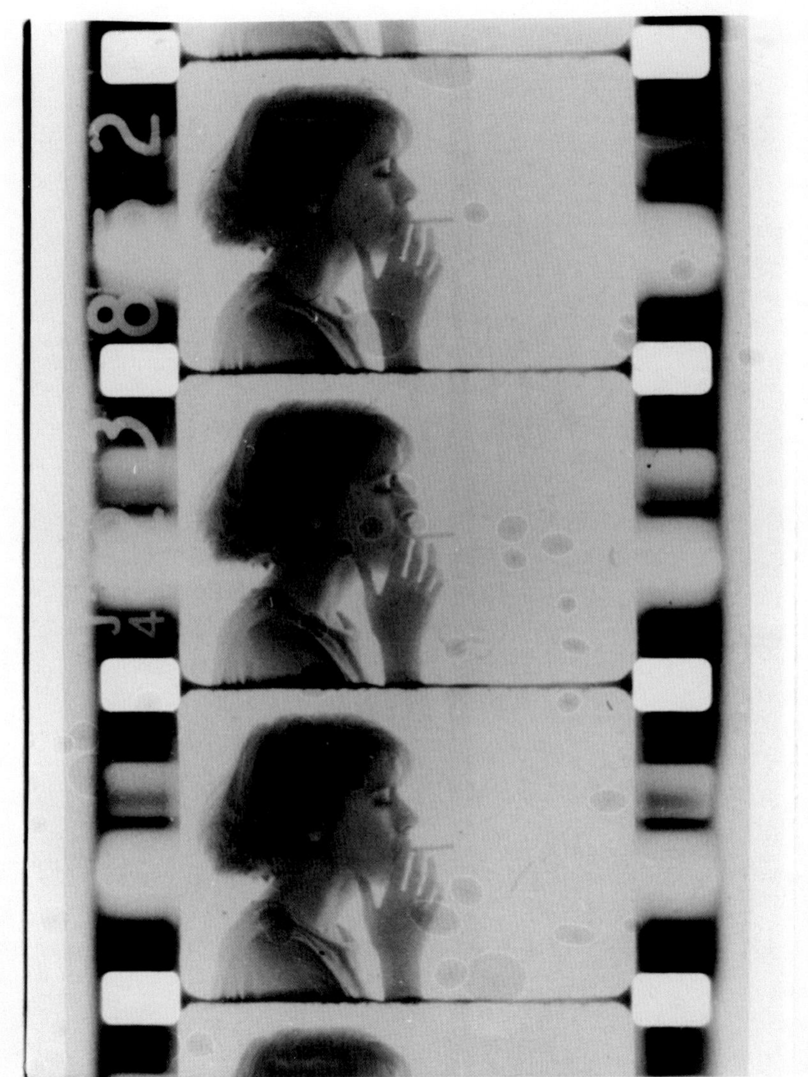

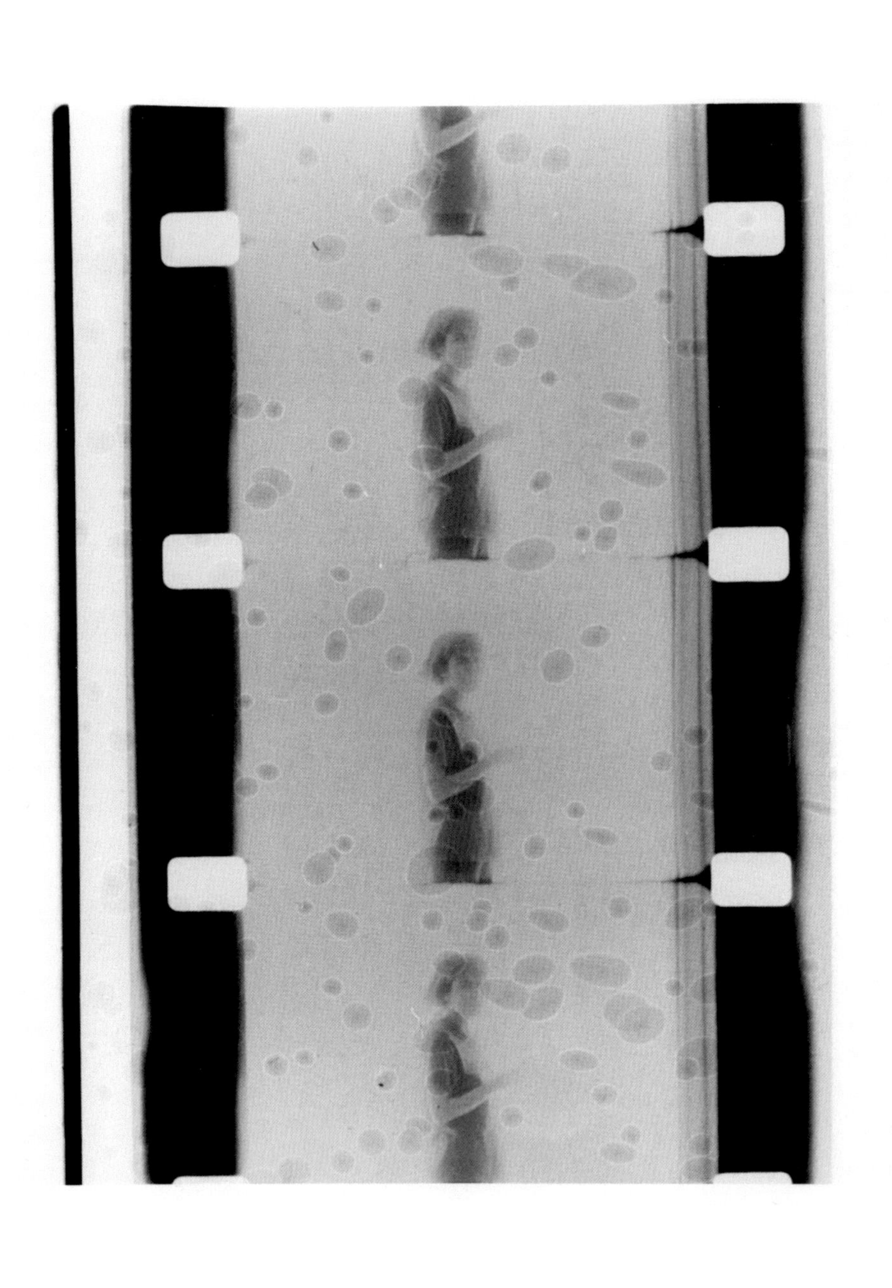

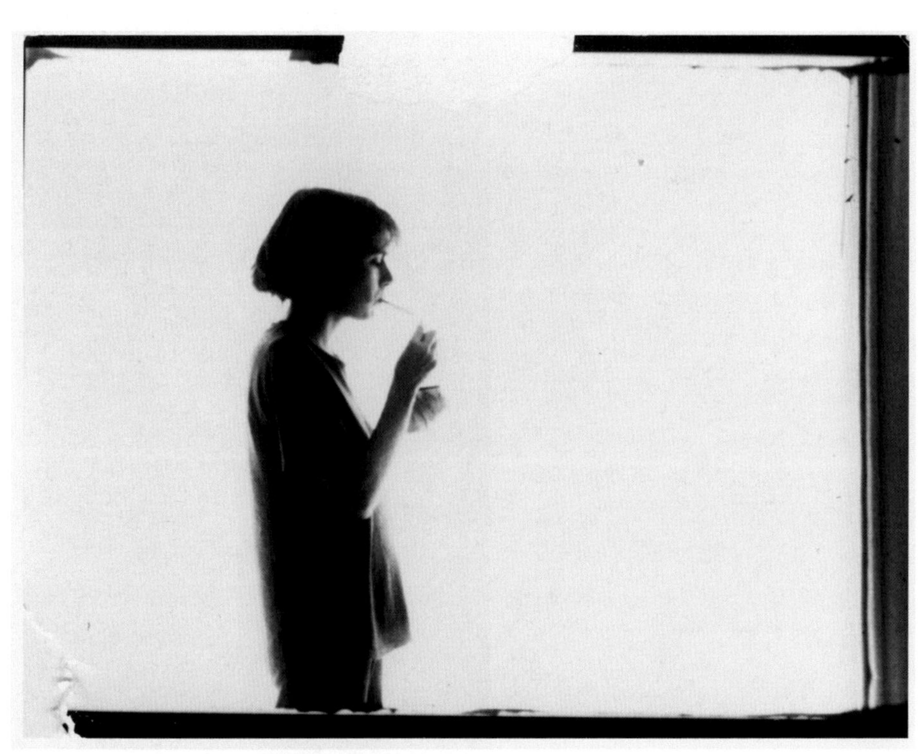

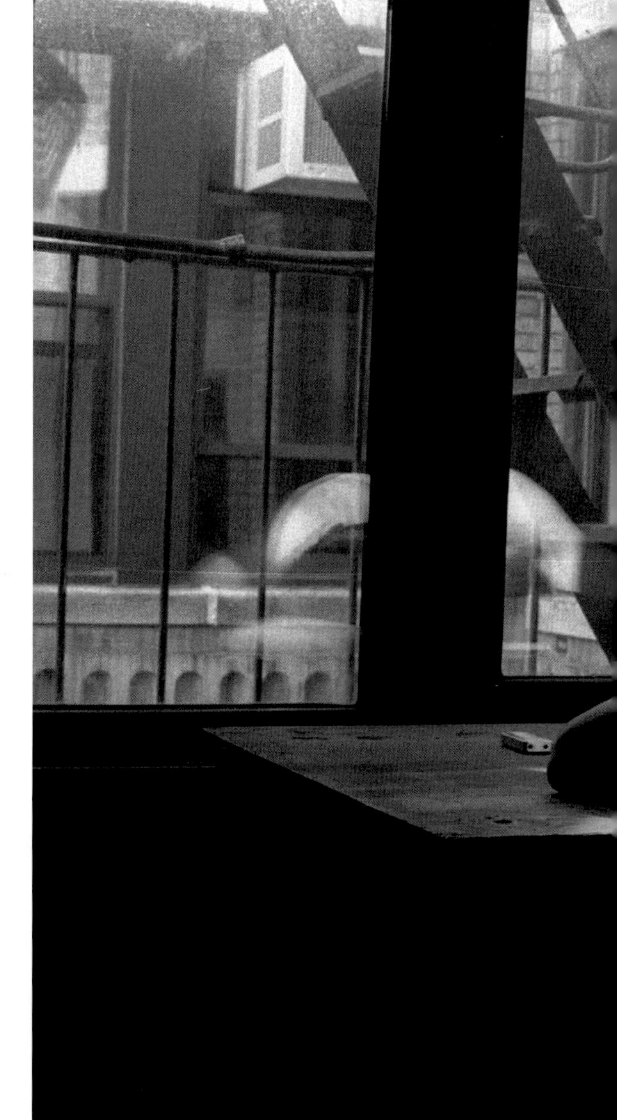

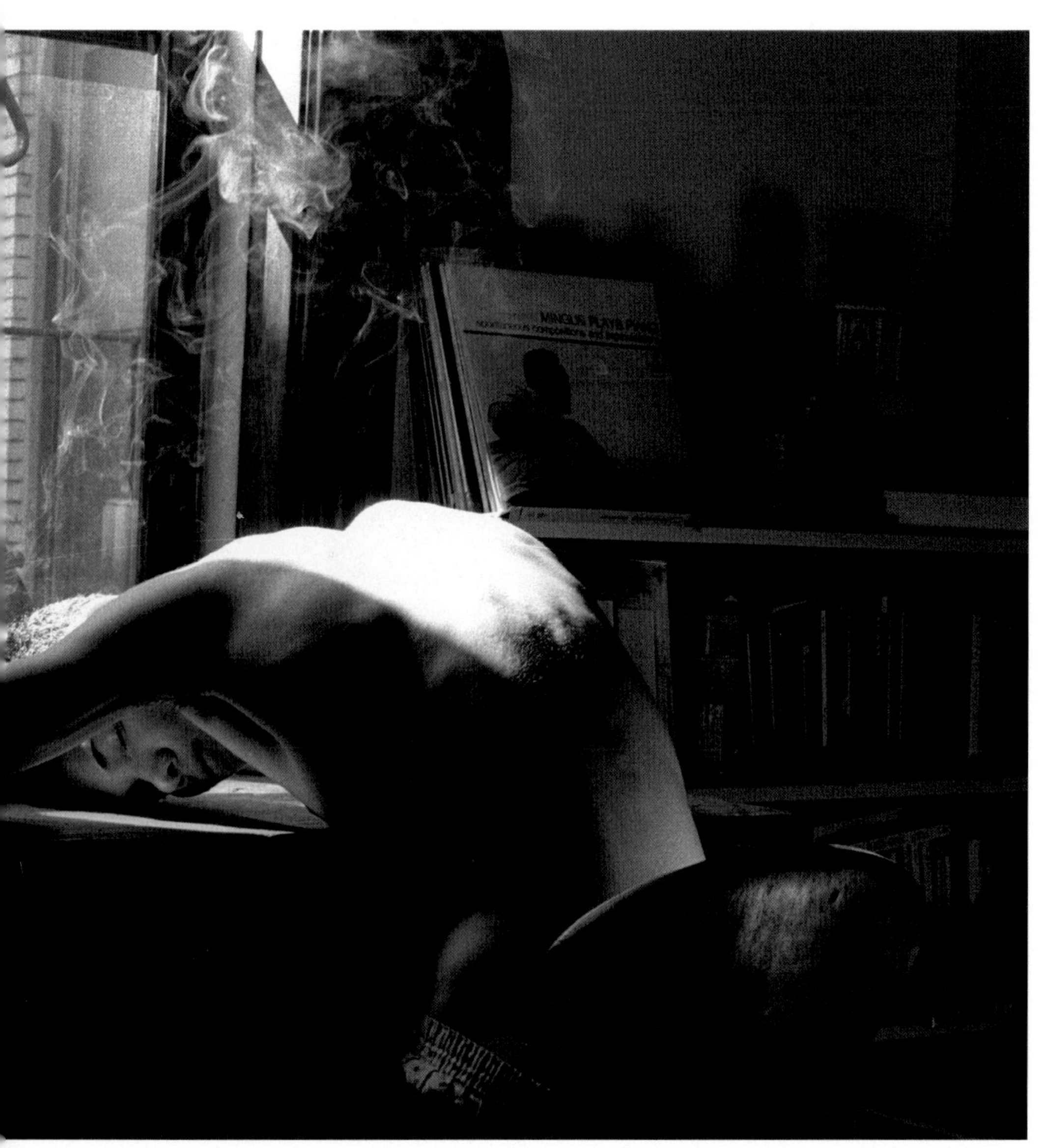
MINGUS PLAYS

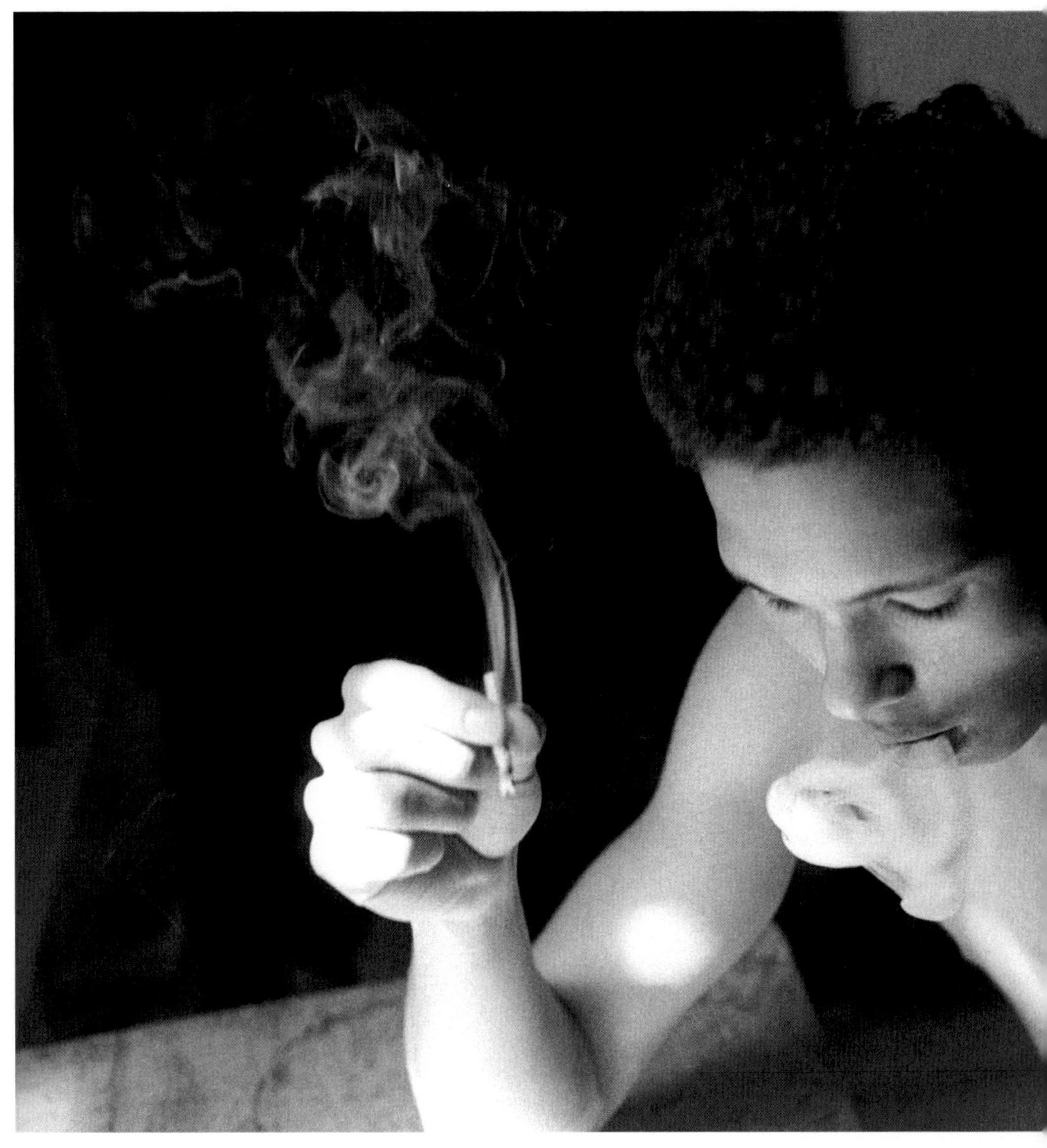

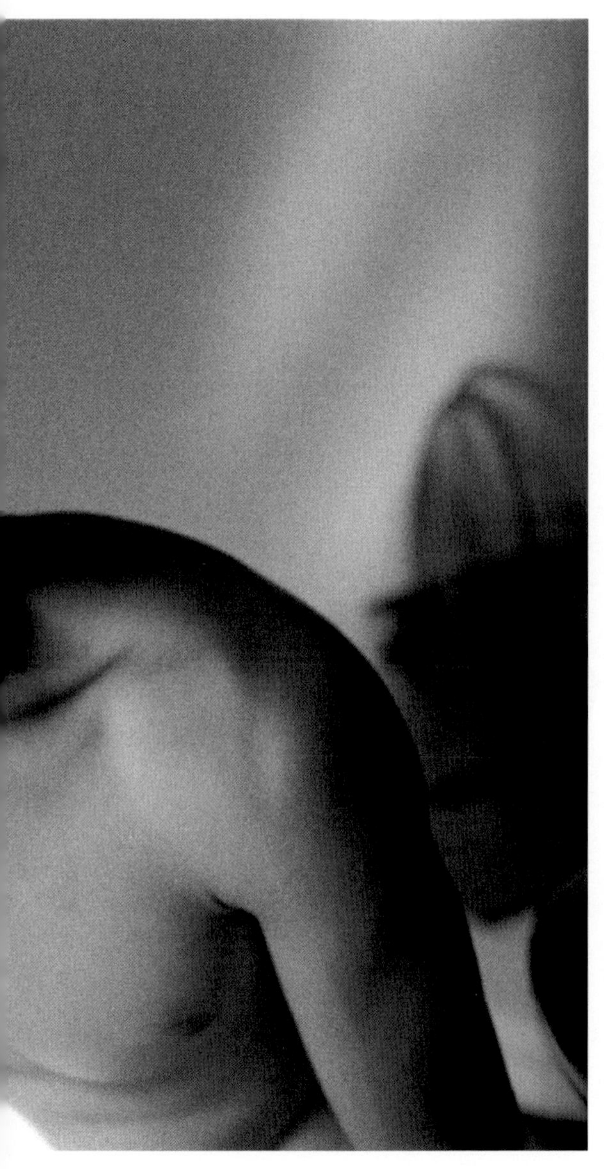

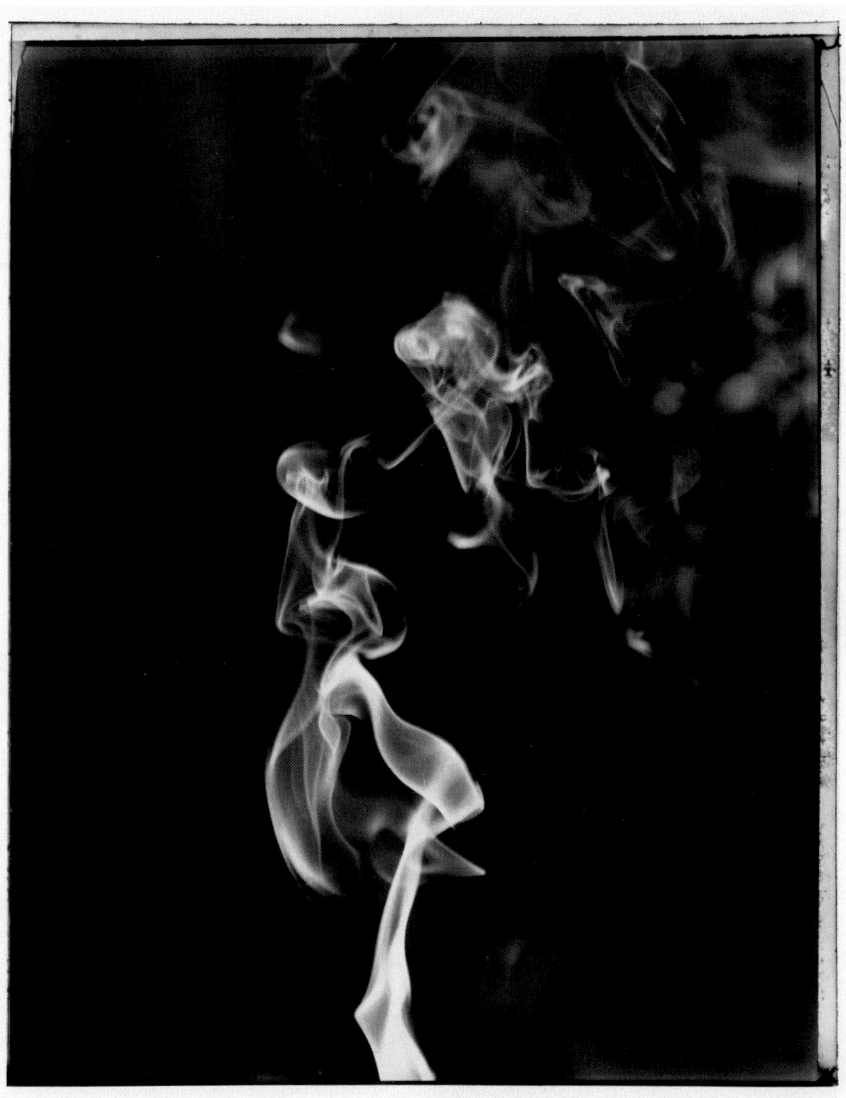

MOYRA DAVEY

Les Goddesses

A young English woman named Mary Wollstonecraft lived by her wits and her pen. At thirty-four, Mary did not expect to marry, but she soon met an American adventurer named Gilbert Imlay and believed she'd found her soul mate. In love, they moved to Paris where they had a daughter, named Fanny.

But Gilbert began to travel more and more, and soon it became apparent he had a wandering eye as well. Heartbroken over this desertion, Mary drank laudanum. She survived, but within a matter of months was despondent again and jumped from a bridge into the Thames.

Miraculously she was rescued and nursed back to health by William Godwin, like Mary a political radical, to whom she quickly developed a strong attachment. Later married and happy, they read Goethe's *The Sorrows of Young Werther* aloud together the night before she went into labor. Tragically, Mary died a few days after giving birth to a second daughter, also named Mary, who would be raised, along with Fanny, by Godwin, who would remarry.

His new wife had a young child of her own, Claire, and the three girls grew up as sisters; they became known as Les Goddesses. When Mary was seventeen, a famous poet named Percy Bysshe Shelley came courting: he first paid favors to Fanny but quickly fell for Mary and the two eloped to Paris, taking Claire with them.

Fanny, crestfallen, stayed behind and, like her mother, drank laudanum. The real story concerning the lives of these extraordinary women is filled with many paradoxes, and without a doubt it is more fantastic than any fiction.

GRAY TO GREEN

Sitting on the floor in sunlight and reading through eight small notebooks going back to 1998, looking for a phrase about Goethe: *The stars above, the plants below.* The thought is connected to Goethe's mother and what she taught him about the natural world; more generally, it is about how people lived in constant relation to nature.

I never found the reference; it was something I had stumbled across on the Internet, but it led me to *The Flight to Italy*, Goethe's diary (recommended by Kafka, in *his* diary), in which G. abruptly takes leave of a turgid existence in Weimar and travels incognito to Italy for the first time in his life. He is thirty-seven years old, and the trip is a revelation and a creative renewal of mammoth proportions. He draws plants, collects rock samples, and begins to dress like the locals so as to pass and be better able to observe their customs. G. reports on the weather patterns (sublime clouds and sunsets); he develops a theory of precipitation involving the curious concept of "elasticity." He looks at architecture and writes of his worshipful love of Palladio; he has a deep appreciation for Italian painting but rails against the squandering of genius and talent on the "senseless . . . stupid subjects" of Christianity.

Because the diary is written quickly, informally, it feels uncannily contemporary. It is hard to believe this is a voice from the late eighteenth century. In addition to studying everything, G. takes a hard look at himself, and toward the end of the book there is a striking revelation: he confesses his "sickness and . . . foolishness," his secret shame that he had never before made the trip to Italy to see firsthand its art and architecture, the objects of his lifelong fascination. Two days before arriving in Rome, he no longer takes off his clothes to sleep so as to hasten his arrival, and on October 26, 1786, he writes, "Next Sunday [I]'ll be sleeping in Rome after 30 years of wishing and hoping."

The effusive diary abruptly goes silent: "I can say nothing now except I am here. . . . Only now do I begin to live." To his Weimar friends, he writes: "I'm here and at peace with myself, and, it seems, at peace with the whole of my life," and to his lover, Charlotte von Stein: "I could spend years here without saying much."

The Flight to Italy is filled with references to plants and crops; G. even has a theory of a "primal plant" form. The only star he mentions, though, is the sun.

THE REAL

Now it is a conflict between the idea of writing from the unknown versus working from notes and journals. Elsewhere, I have compared these different modes of writing to two genres in photography: the vérité approach of the street, seizing life and movement with little chance of reprise, and, in contrast, the controlled practice of the studio, where the artist is less exposed, the environment more forgiving, and time more malleable. And perhaps another iteration of this distinction between risk and control was intimated in something I heard a critic, quoting Godard, say on the radio when I lived in Paris in 2008: "Filmmakers who make installations instead of films are afraid of the Real."

In his six-hour documentary *Phantom India*, Louis Malle travels all over the subcontinent filming, and later, in voice-over, he analyzes and reflects on the intrusion and indiscretion of the camera. Malle will never get over this feeling of impropriety, but he will keep on shooting, hour after hour, pushing up against the act of documentary in an attempt to understand something about India and something about himself. Much of *Phantom India* is straight-up documentary, but there are moments of intense self-scrutiny and questioning, for instance when Malle describes his inability to be "present," to experience the "Real" of what is taking place before the camera.

He lives in his head, sometimes thinking of the past but mostly caught up in a work whose meaning will only be locked in at a future moment. To every new situation, his first instinct is to invoke memory and analysis: a scene on a beach at daybreak reminds him of another, twenty years earlier, when he was making his first film. "A tamer of time, a slave of time" is how Malle understands his predicament. At a certain point, he and his crew stop filming. Only then do they begin to experience the present tense, the slowness of time, and what Malle calls the Real.

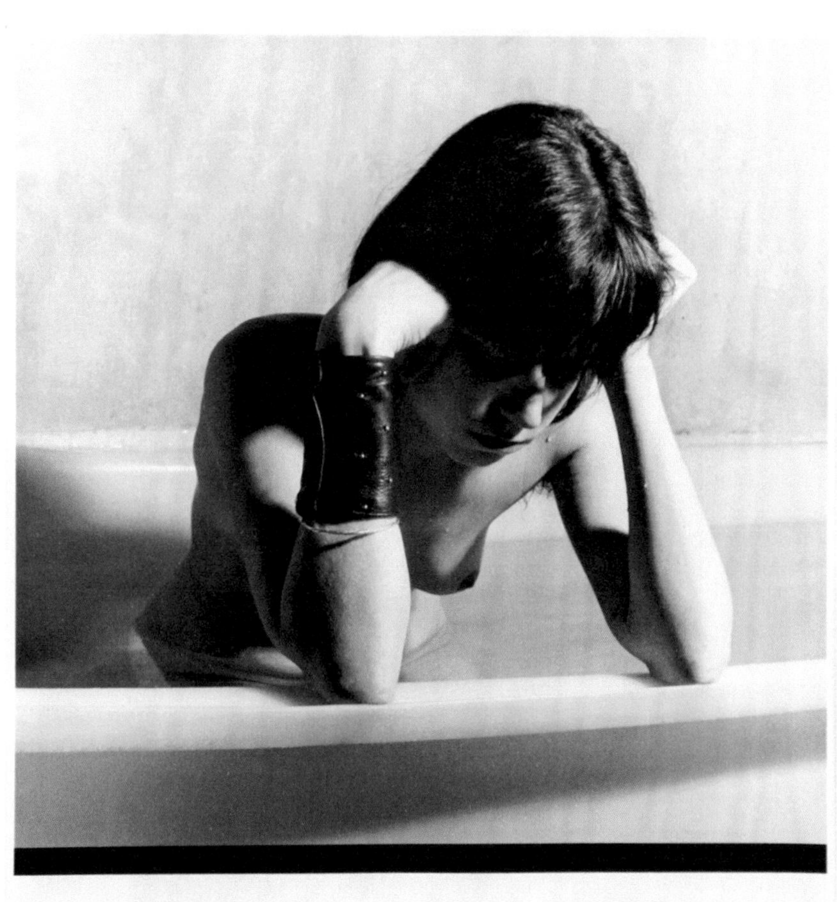

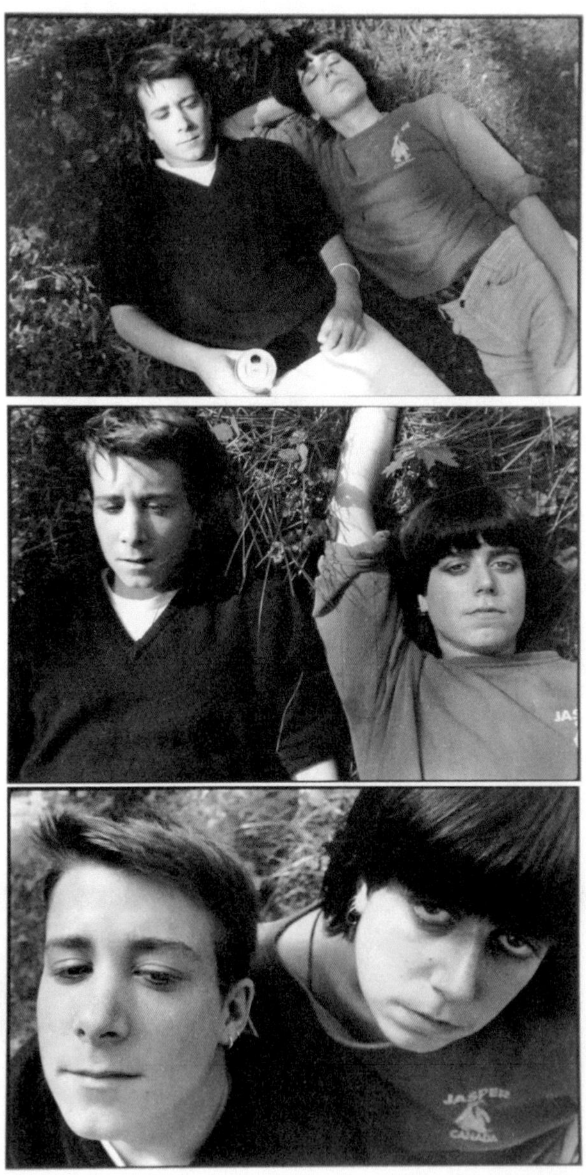
JASPER
CANADA

THE WET

Another problem for me now is the welling up of the "Wet," the insistent preoccupation with narrating certain aspects of the discredited past, things I may never be ready to tell.

Previously I have incited myself to write by beginning with the most pressing thing, but the problem now is that I can't face writing about the Wet. I think about giving it a masquerade, or perhaps the Wet will duly give way to something else.

This document parallels another one written from notes collected in diaries. That one is accompanied by the uneasy feeling of cannibalizing myself. *This* document, though not a book, is trying to begin according to a principle described by Marguerite Duras: "To be without a subject for a book, without any idea of a book, is to find yourself in front of a book. An immense void. An eventual book. In front of writing, live and naked, something terrible to surmount." I wanted to try, almost as an experiment, to write both ways, one alongside the other in tandem, but already I've begun to fold in notes from that other document . . .

Was Duras opening her veins? Yes and no. She was also opening the bottle. But she would go at it—writing and drinking—for days and nights. She had stamina, as Susan Sontag would say. And she was not afraid of the Wet.

Rainer Werner Fassbinder: "The more honestly you put yourself into the story, the more that story will concern others as well."

MARY

Mary Wollstonecraft, born in 1759, ten years after Goethe and two hundred years before my sister Claire, was Wet and Dry. She was a brilliant star in her firmament, a passionate early advocate of women's, children's, and human rights, and an enlightened defender of truth and justice: a radical. She went to Paris to witness the revolution and lived to tell of the bloody Terror of 1793–94. A woman with enormous intellectual capabilities and savoir faire, she supported herself, and at various times one or more of her largely hapless six siblings, by writing.

But she also suffered from depression and, brokenhearted over the rejection by Imlay, drank laudanum. In an attempt to revive her, he offered a mission of travel to Scandinavia to investigate a murky business affair of his. Mary accepted because she needed the money and hoped that this continued involvement with Imlay might ensure a positive romantic outcome.

In 1795, she set out on a dangerous ocean voyage with her infant daughter, Fanny, and a French maid. Like Goethe on his travels to Italy, Wollstonecraft wrote letters to Imlay chronicling her observations and emotional responses to the landscape and peoples of Sweden, Norway, and Denmark. Her heartbreak is softly intimated in the letters, but mostly she reflects and reports with a journalist's eye on the native customs: a featherbed so soft and deep it is like "sinking into the grave"; children swaddled in heavy, insalubrious layers of flannel; airless homes heated with stoves instead of fires—here, like Goethe, Mary invokes the odd concept of "elasticity" to talk about the air. Viewing the mummified remains of some nobles, she responds with characteristic indignation: "When I was shewn these human petrefactions, I shrunk back with disgust and horror. 'Ashes to ashes!' thought I—'Dust to dust!'"

After her return home to England, Wollstonecraft composed the letters into an extremely well-received book titled *Letters Written during a Short Residence in Sweden, Norway, and Denmark.* It was published in 1796, two hundred years before the birth of my son, Barney.

ALISON

Soon after I arrived in Paris, shaky with jet lag and insomnia, I asked Alison, my oldest friend, if she'd help me brainstorm. Bless her, she is always willing, and she is a font of ideas and strategies. I was struggling and fearful, convinced I'd do nothing of value in this city: I took a pill and drank a glass of wine on a cold terrace on the rue de Rivoli, and told Alison this: "I came to Paris in 1976 just out of high school. I was lonely, depressed, bored, illiterate. I was thin, I was fat, with no control over any of it. I was a Francophile with a deep longing to be part of the culture, but I was clueless, infused with teenage ideas about 'the Romantic.' A French friend told me emphatically: 'the Romantic is the nineteenth century. End of story.' I met the two Quebecois artists in the Cité Internationale des Arts studios. They were friendly but aloof. Thirty years later, I am back in Paris with a husband, a son, a life. I have one of those studios. I am thin. I have money. I have MS." Alison's eyes lit up: "*That* is the perfect story." But I have no idea how to write a story. About telling certain episodes of your past, Norman Mailer said: "You must be ready." I may never be ready. Some excised paragraphs, the original motivation for this project, now reside in a separate document labeled "Pathography."

Why does everyone want to tell their story? Why do all of my students talk about "representing memory"? Why is Amy, in grad school, suddenly conscious of her working-class roots, destabilized, and obsessed with her childhood? Why is my sister Jane tormented by the past and asking Mom to talk to her shrink? Why did I spend so much time in Paris, agoraphobic, brooding, tunneling into realms of childhood where I found pockets of it illuminated with sudden, violent flashes?

Hannah Arendt, quoting Isak Dinesen: "The reward of storytelling is to be able to let go. . . . 'All sorrows can be borne if you put them into a story or tell a story about them.'"

SIBLINGS

At the end of my copy of *Flight to Italy*, there are short bios of all the principals in Goethe's life. His mother, Catharina Elisabeth von Goethe, is described as a very supportive woman, and there is a citation from Freud about G. having been his mother's favorite and about how children singled out in this way retain a lifelong confidence and glow. This led me to Freud's brief essay "A Childhood Recollection," an analysis of an early memory G. recounts in his autobiography of throwing dishes out the window when he was a small child. The episode remained mysterious to Freud until, as is typical of his method, he began to hear similar stories from his patients and started to piece together a theory, namely that the throwing of objects out the window is typically linked to a child's fury and jealousy in response to the arrival of a new baby. I strongly suspect I reacted just as violently or even more so to the births of my five younger siblings. A therapist explained this to me once and said I should practice self-forgiveness, but it took Freud's words to cement the

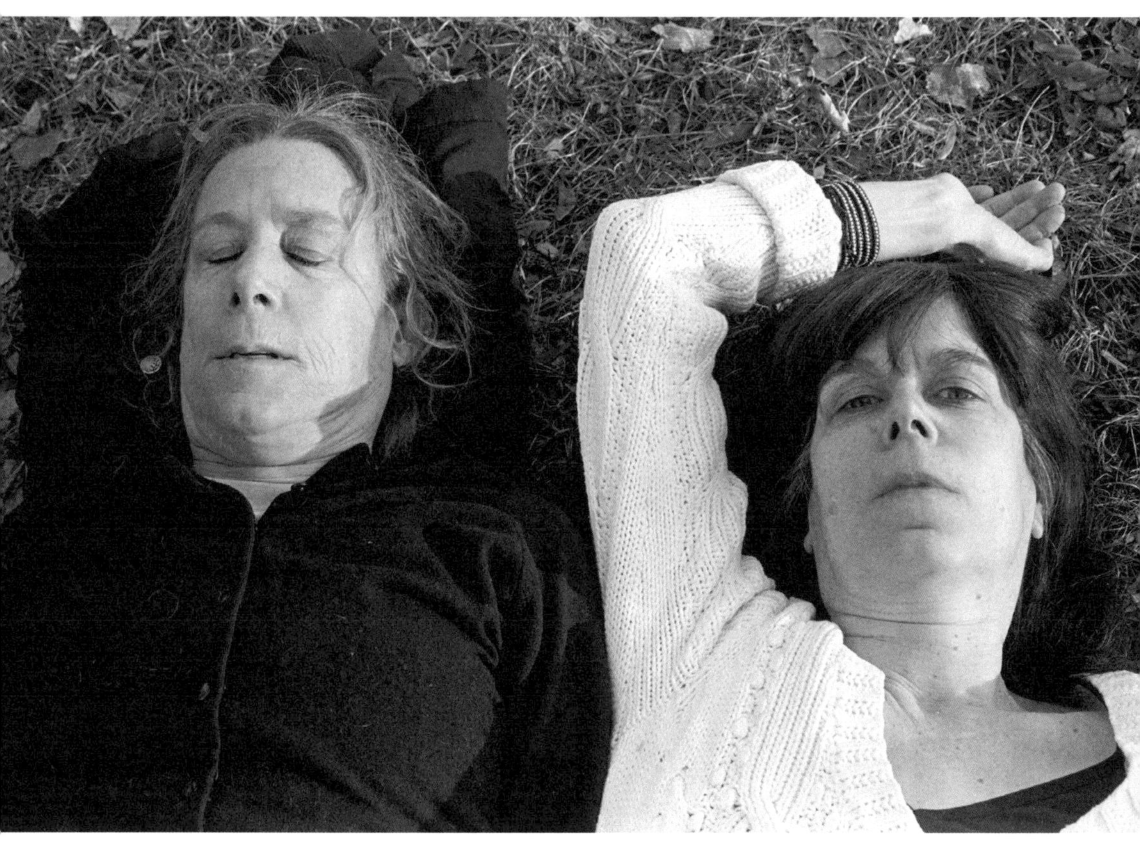

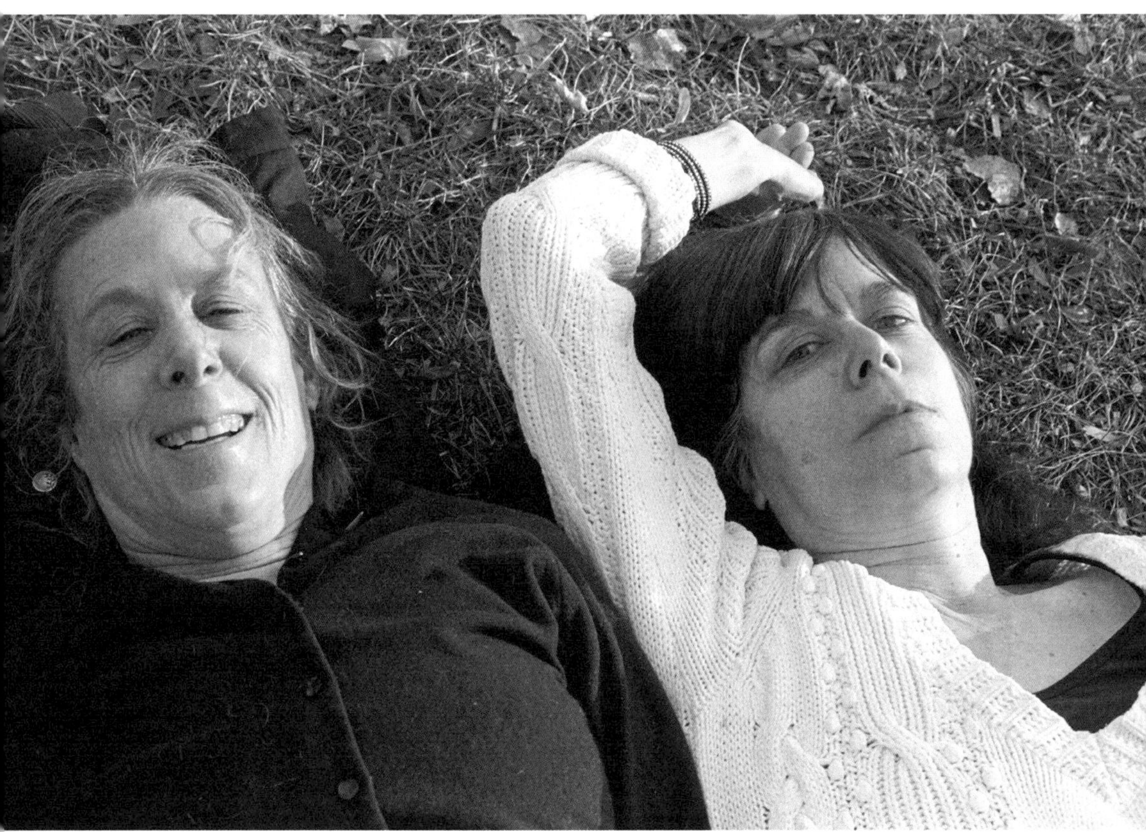

notion that my behavior was not a murderous aberration of childhood. A description of one of these cruel episodes of "acting out" has been excised and relegated to the "Pathography."

Michael Haneke: "Artists don't need shrinks because they can work it out in their work."

But can we do without Freud?

SHARON & GLORIA

I fell asleep in the afternoon and dreamed I was commiserating with Sharon Hayes about how a work, once finished, is "like a tombstone." Gloria Naylor said this about her book *The Women of Brewster Place*: "I had gotten a bound copy of the book—which I really call a tombstone because that's what it represents, at least for my part of the experience."

The thing is only alive (and, by extension, *I* am only alive) while it is in process, and I've never quite figured out how to keep it ignited, moving. Some stubborn gene always threatens to flood the engine just at the crucial moment of shifting gears.

MARY & MARY

Like Goethe's *Flight*, Wollstonecraft's *Letters*, a narrative moderated by a journey, has a special, self-generating momentum: a trip, with its displacements in time and space, can be the perfect way to frame a story. Combine this with an epistolary address, and it would appear to be the most easeful of forms. *Letters* was the only happy outcome of the Scandinavian trip. Five months after her first suicide attempt, on confirmation that

Imlay had a lover, Mary jumped from a bridge in rain-soaked clothing to hasten her descent. She was saved by a boatman and briefly consoled by Imlay, who shortly thereafter disappeared for good from the lives of Mary and Fanny. But M. W. was lucky to find a friend in the person of William Godwin, a sage man who, according to M. W. biographer Lyndall Gordon, counseled: "A disappointed woman should try to construct happiness 'out of a set of materials within [her] reach.'"

A year later, in 1797, in love with Godwin, married, and pregnant, Mary read Goethe's *The Sorrows of Young Werther* aloud with William. The following night, she went into labor and gave birth to a child who would grow up to be Mary Shelley, whom she would soon leave motherless. The delivery was botched: the placenta did not descend, and a doctor's unwashed hands reached into the womb to tear it out. Sepsis set in, the mother's milk became infected, and puppies were used to draw off lactation. Two hundred years later, in 1997, less than six months after giving birth, I flew across North America with an electric pump to suction the milk from my breasts. But I missed my connection and arrived at my destination twelve hours later, my breasts grotesquely engorged. I took a photo in the hotel room and some years later published it in *LTTR*, a minutely circulating queer-feminist journal. Now that photo is all over the Internet, completely out of my control.

Part of the tragic irony of M. W.'s death in childbirth was her own enlightened advocacy of simple hygiene and nonintervention in the care of infants and mothers; suspicious of doctors, she was a believer in wholesomeness and common sense in an age of superstition and quackery.

THE SUN

Wollstonecraft and Goethe, both northerners from cold, rainy climates, enthused repeatedly in their correspondences about the presence of sunshine. Goethe marveled to his friends about its perpetual abundance in Italy ("these skies, where all day long you don't have to give a thought to your body"), and for Wollstonecraft in Scandinavia its effects were central to her evocation of the sublime, which she experienced in her travels along the rocky coast and mountainous landscapes of Sweden and Norway.

The warm reach of the sun was also surely a factor in granting each of them a measure of peace: for Goethe, when he arrives in Rome and no longer feels the need to double his life in writing ("I am here. . . . Only now do I begin to live"), and for Wollstonecraft, during countless moments when nature impresses itself on her as the salve and renewal of an exhausted, disillusioned spirit. Waking on a ship one morning, she greets daybreak with these words: "I opened my bosom to the embraces of nature; and my soul rose to its author." Two decades later, her daughter Mary Shelley would write from the banks of Lake Geneva: "When the sun bursts forth it is with a splendour and heat unknown in England."

In 2004, in Needville, Texas, an asteroid was named for Mary Wollstonecraft (Minor Planet Center designation 90481 Wollstonecraft).

"LES GODDESSES"

Aaron Burr, visiting England from America in 1812, bestowed this epithet on Mary Wollstonecraft's daughters, Fanny and

Mary, and their stepsister, Clara Mary Jane Clairmont, known then as Jane and later as Claire. Two years hence, Mary, age seventeen, and Percy Bysshe Shelley eloped to France with Jane in tow; Fanny—with disastrous results—was not invited to join them. Lord Byron soon formed part of the group, and together they lived an idyll of poetry, song, travel, and love, surviving on whatever money they could squeeze from Shelley's father. On foot, atop a donkey, and by boat, they journeyed through parts of France, Switzerland, and Germany, keeping a collective diary subsequently published under the title *History of a Six Weeks' Tour.* Nearly two hundred years later, I procured a facsimile edition of this book printed in New Delhi, no doubt downloaded from Google Books: the insides are a distant cousin of the original typeset, but the cover is a bright red design adorned with Islamic patterning. It is an utterly charming object, as is the prose it contains.

Eventually, the Shelleys settled in Italy, where they wrote; read the classics, Rousseau, and Goethe; and Jane, in particular, studied music and languages. About Rome, Mary proclaimed: "[It] has such an effect on me that my past life before I saw it appears a blank & now I begin to live." They existed like this for eight years, short of money, outcasts living in defiance of the rigid matrimonial conventions of the early nineteenth century. The ménage was not without its tensions and jealousies: Mary, pregnant and ill for much of the time, quickly began to find Jane (now Claire) an irritant. Claire was vivacious and talented, and though she could sometimes be dispatched, she would remain a resolute fixture of the Shelley circle. Mary began to use a little sun symbol in her diary to indicate Claire's presence on any given day. ☼

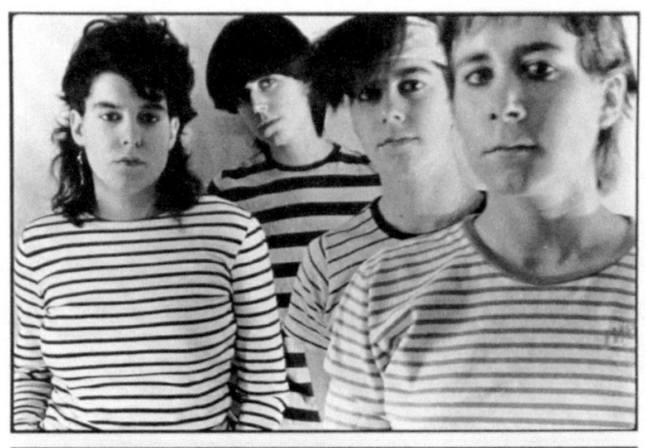

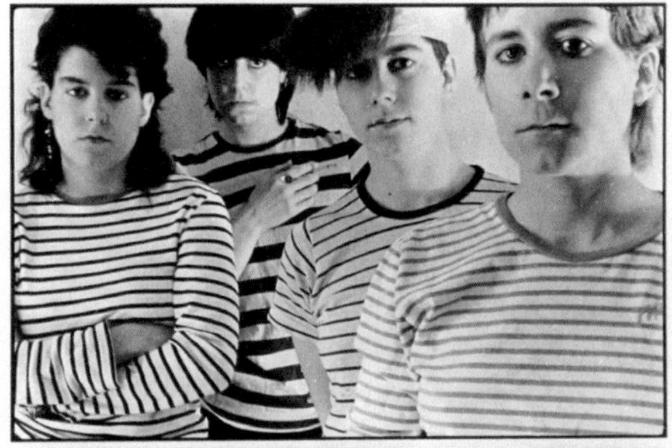

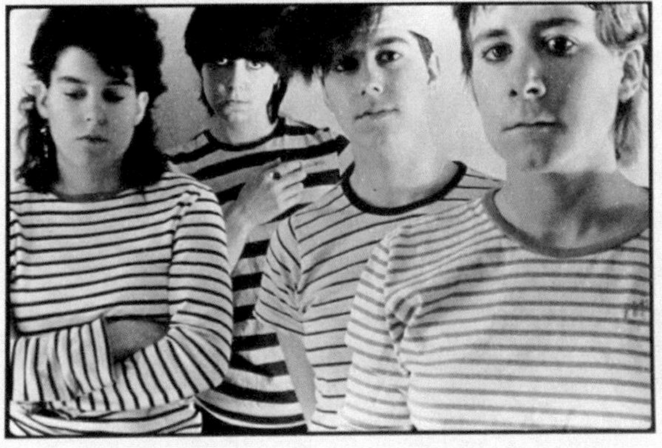

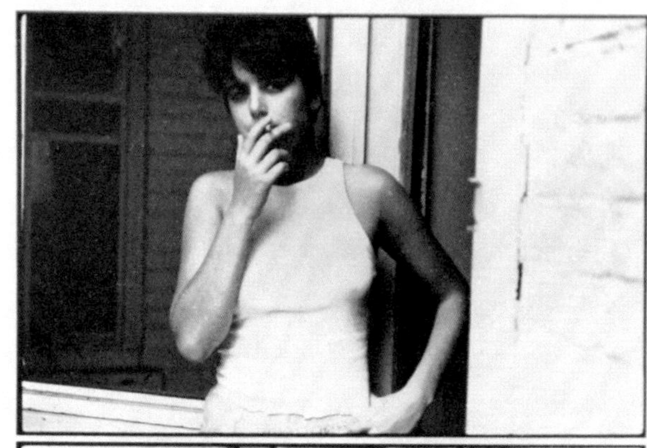

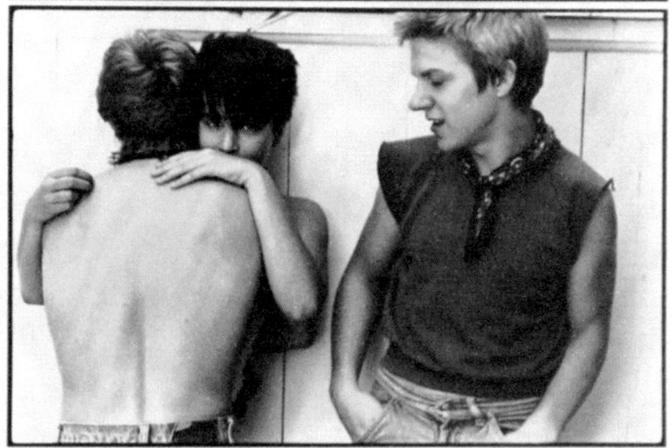

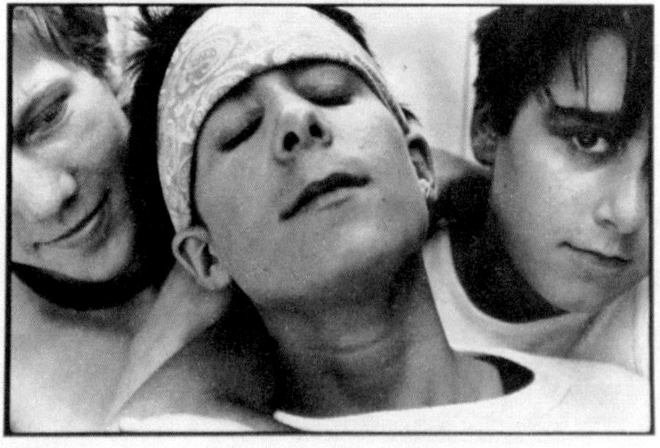

JANE

Mary Wollstonecraft's parents, John Edward and Elizabeth, were married in 1756; their union produced seven children. Two hundred years later, in 1956, my parents, James and Patricia, met in England and married. They also had seven children—six girls and one boy—beginning with Jane Elisabeth in 1957.

Prompted by a stay in rehab, my sister decided to write a memoir of her childhood and addiction. In an e-mail, she told me: "I am in the process of teasing out an ending, but I'm now edging up to a very respectable 60,000 words, plenty to qualify for a book. Now, of course, that the deed is nearing completion and *I have set down once and for all a true record of what has happened* (sorta, kinda), I am feeling somewhat uncertain."

M. W. wrote of "the healing balm of sympathy [as the] medicine of life," a concept Jane, an uncommonly sensitive and empathic person—always, since childhood—and now an amateur homeopath, would undoubtedly agree with. Jane reminds me of M. W. in some ways. A nurturing mother of three daughters, she is a strong and caring woman who, like M. W. at times, both keeps her distance from doctors and their drugs and is emotionally fragile, prone to depression and occasional rash behavior.

FANNY

Fanny, to whom Percy Shelley had first shown affection, was excluded from the Summer of Love. She had inherited her mother's melancholic streak, and though she tried to combat the depressive feelings she was dogged by what she called

"Spleen. Indolence. Torpor. Ill-humour." Fannykin—of whom Mary Wollstonecraft wrote in the Scandinavian *Letters* when her child was a babe, "I dread lest she should be forced to sacrifice her heart to her principles, or her principles to her heart"—succumbed to exactly that predicament of the nineteenth-century woman without means. Fearful of becoming a burden, Fanny drank laudanum as her mother had done, but unlike Mary, she was successful.

Young Mary's bliss with Shelley was short-lived, as death began to intrude with frightening regularity. Of her four pregnancies, only one child, Percy Florence, survived. Claire's daughter by Byron, Allegra, whom Byron callously separated from her mother, died at age five, alone in an Italian convent. Just prior, Claire had written heartbreakingly in her journal that recovering Allegra would be like "com[ing] back to the warm ease of life after the coldness and stiffness of the grave." Shelley's first wife, Harriet, in an advanced state of pregnancy, drowned herself in 1816, and eight years into his relationship with Mary, Shelley himself drowned in a boating accident on the Gulf of La Spezia off the coast of Pisa with their close friend Edward Williams. Byron, who'd committed himself to a war of independence in Greece, died two years later in Missolonghi of fever.

JAMES & PATRICIA

In 1975, my father, James, aged forty-five, fell from the roof of our house one Saturday morning in August and never regained consciousness. I had just turned seventeen, the same age as Mary Wollstonecraft Godwin when she eloped to France with Percy Bysshe Shelley and Jane Clairmont. My mother, Patricia, retreated to the top of our big box of a house and all hell broke loose below. The Davey girls were not writing poetry, studying Greek and Latin, and procreating; we were listening to David Bowie, Roxy Music, and the Clash and ingesting too many drugs. Interviewed by a journalist friend about our active sex lives at the time, my mother responded ruefully: "I'd mind less if I thought they enjoyed it more." It was a different time and different kind of rebellion; nonetheless, many thought of us as a female force—goddesses, no, but "Amazonian," yes, to be reckoned with. And that is what I tried to show in a series of portraits I took in Ottawa and Montreal beginning around 1980. "Les jeunes filles en fleur" was another expression used by the same journalist friend to describe some of us, but that came later, after we'd settled down a bit.

CLAIRE & KATE

Claire Davey, small and taut, and the only one among us who did not regularly swell and shrink, never succumbed to intoxicants or liquor. And she never threw herself at men, as did some of her sisters, as did Claire Clairmont with Byron. Temperate, she traveled, she studied; now she teaches philosophy and yoga to high school students in Toronto. Kate, born a year and a half after Claire, in 1961, two hundred years after Mary's brother Henry Wollstonecraft, was the fearless party girl, drinking and inhaling pills until she passed out. Kate never "recovered" into anything resembling normalcy. Multiple stays in rehab would eventually lead to a lifetime of AA, NA, OA. Intelligent, sensitive, she opted out. She read every novel on my mother's bookshelves and filled the house with rescued animals. Some of the original five cats and four dogs have passed on, but the smells linger to remind us of nineteen-year-old, blind, incontinent Candy and gentle, gormless, clubfooted Duke, found on a reservation.

CLAIRE

Of the Shelley entourage, only Mary; her son, Percy; and Claire Clairmont lived beyond their thirties. At the dissolution of their circle, Claire joined her brother in Vienna and began to work as a teacher, but she was hounded out of this employment by the lingering scandal of her youth and forced to migrate as far as Moscow, where she became a governess. Her journal, a penetrating literary document, was published a century later; an old woman, she eventually settled in Florence with her niece Paola and became the model for Henry James's story *The Aspern Papers.*

MARY & PERCY

Widowed, Mary Shelley was at the mercy of her tyrannical and conservative father-in-law, a man who had never accepted his son's poetic gift, nor his marriage to Mary. After editing a posthumous collection of Shelley's work in 1824, Mary was forbidden by the patriarch from publishing any more of Shelley's poetry or even writing about him, lest it shame the family, thus forcing her into a conventional lifestyle for the sake of her son and his inheritance, small sums of which were parsed out to them while Shelley senior lived on and on, defying all expectations of his demise.

According to Muriel Spark, Percy Florence inherited none of his parents' literary or artistic talent and refused to visit art museums with his mother when they traveled in Europe. He was a disappointment to Mary, but she later grew to appreciate what Spark termed his "phlegmatic qualities." Percy was "to remain loyally and negatively by [Mary's] side to sustain her old age." He married Jane Gibson, a sympathetic woman who

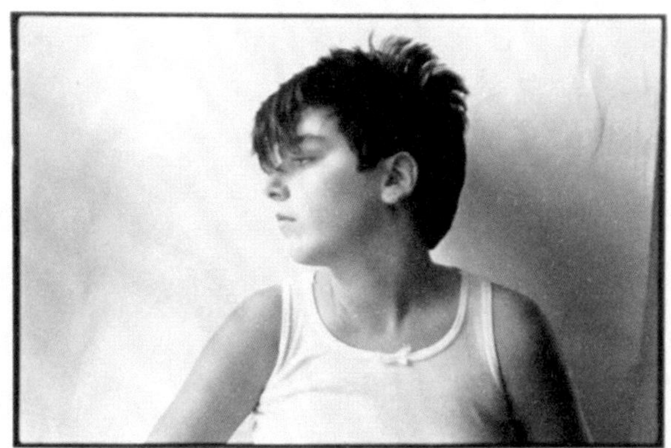

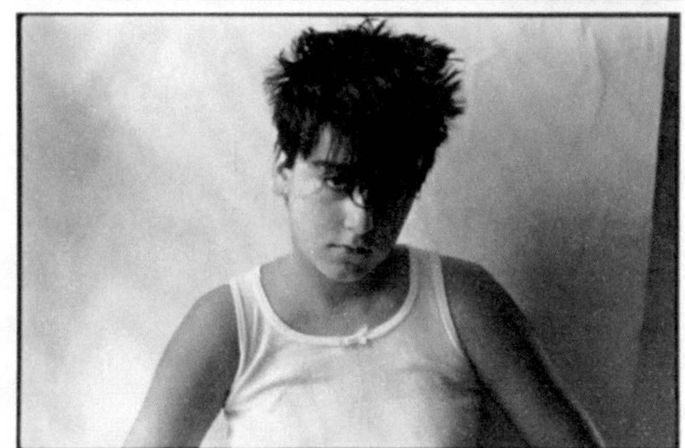

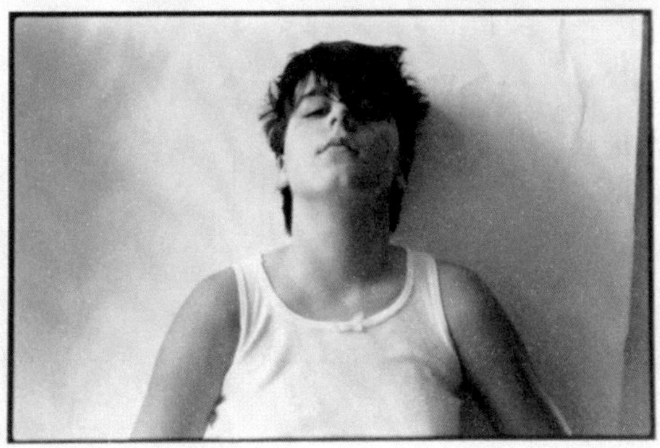

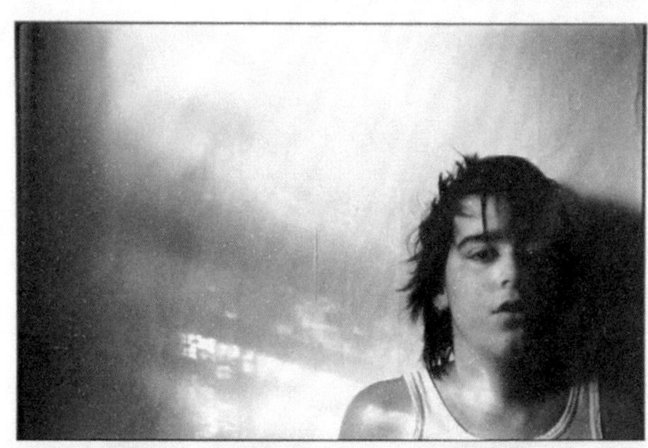

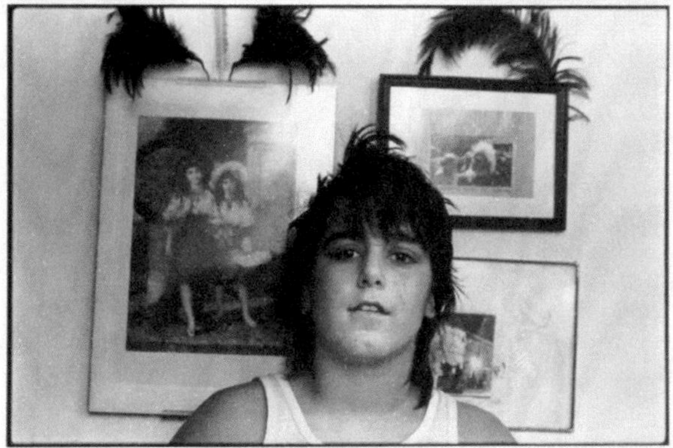

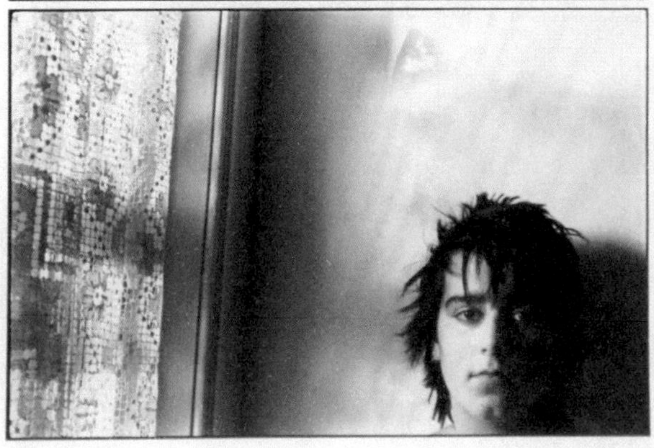

became Mary's friend and caretaker during her final illness at age fifty-three. Percy and Jane did not have children.

BARNEY

Age thirteen, Barney does not like art museums either—he says they instantly make him feel sleepy. He told me, "An ideal way to spend the day would be to drive to an airport and watch the planes take off and land."

TAUTOLOGY

I learned the meaning of this from Baudelaire via Barthes: "I take H [hashish] in order to be free. But in order to take H I must already be free." And from Alejandra Pizarnik: "To not eat I must be happy. And I cannot be happy if I am fat." This comes close to summing up my adolescence.

HOMEOPATHY

In November 2010, on the recommendation of my sister Jane, I traveled to Montreal to visit Dr. Saine, a famous homeopath, a man who, like his father before him, had treated thousands of people with MS. I sat with him in his Dickensian study, surrounded by stacks of paper and books, some framing white busts—no doubt Dr. Saine's predecessors, the discoverers of this strange and mystical science. He interviewed me for three and a half hours about symptoms, cravings, fears, and dreams. He felt my frozen feet and lit a fire, burning a cube of oak. "How do you feel when you see a poor person? On a scale of one to ten, how much do you fear poverty? Cancer? Death?" "How do you feel when you are with your son and your husband enters the room?" And on and on. "Is there anything you haven't told me about yourself?" I told as much as I could, including some of the bad and shameful memories from the "Pathography" (because you have to), but the long interview was tiring, and my fragmented story came out rather flat and monotone. He received it all without judgment, indeed, with a high degree of curiosity, almost excitement.

He said my case was unusual—perhaps my parental influences were too strong, too dominant, neither one giving way—and this left him torn between two antidotes. I departed with two tiny glass vials, coincidently each substance related to photography: sepia, which is a dye used to tone photographic prints, and lycopodium, the spores of club mosses that were ground into combustible powder and ignited in the era before flashbulbs.

BEING

"To do without people is for photography the most impossible of renunciations," wrote Walter Benjamin. Yet that abandonment is precisely what would begin to take place in my photographs over the next ten years, beginning in 1984, until my subjects constituted little more than the dust on my bookshelves or the view under the bed. The burden of image theft, as Louis Malle put it, had something to do with my retreat, but also a gradual seeping in of a kind of biographical reticence, perhaps connected to my present reservations around telling my story ("Pathography").

I, too, ingested excessive substances in decades two and three, and one result is that I can barely keep track of the analogies

I've posited, from Duras's "immense void" and the unscripted of vérité, between rehearsed writing (from journals) and photographic mise-en-scène. And what is meant by the Real in the pronouncements of Malle and Godard ("Filmmakers who make installations instead of films are afraid of the Real")? For Godard, the Real is about confrontation and risk in time-based media, the old-fashioned way, no props allowed. Malle uses the term to describe a state of "being" to which he accedes when he finally stops filming in India; it is about experiencing a kind of existential peace, a freedom from the need to be making something. But he can only enjoy the feeling because he has worked very hard for it.

THE GREEN & THE WET

Over the years, I've brushed up against a peculiar sensation of "being," usually in green places where water infuses the air: in a marshy field in England crisscrossed by canals; on the tiny, narrow peninsula of pine-choked soil that is Provincetown, in fall or winter. Something about the "elasticity" of the air infuses "the elasticity of my spirits" and allows me to enter an unusual state of weightlessness, an intense and rare feeling of well-being.

Displacement in space, and the attendant fatigue of travel, must be contributing factors to this febrile state, not unrelated to Stendhal syndrome, which had its origins in Florence in 1817. Stendhal noted this phenomenon in Italy just one year before Claire Clairmont and the Shelley party found themselves climbing the ruins of the Colosseum on their nightly walks through Rome. Goethe, Mary Wollstonecraft, and the Shelleys were all weary travelers—M. W. had recently given birth, and Mary Shelley, her daughter, was more or less pregnant for five years. They both had very young children in tow; they were exhausted. In early 1997, sleep deprived, I walked through the snow-covered woods of Provincetown with infant Barney strapped to my chest. I needed to move at all costs; I craved something mind-altering.

SEPIA DAYS

Mary Shelley died in 1851 and Claire Clairmont in 1879, but no photographs of them seem to exist, at least on the Web; there is a photographic oval of Percy Florence Shelley as an older man—he looks a bit like Freud.

In his essay "A Little History of Photography," Walter Benjamin cites Goethe, apropos of August Sander: "There is a delicate empiricism which so intimately involves itself with the object that it becomes true theory." Mary Wollstonecraft and Goethe were just prephotography, Goethe by only seven years. Their travel writings have the vividness and spontaneity of snapshots, and Goethe's phrases and sketches, in particular, feel startlingly modern. It is not a stretch to imagine that Goethe, with his scientific mind, might have anticipated the nascent technology: it was "in the air," after all, long before 1839.

The close observation that Goethe championed and was his means to knowledge, to "true theory," was precisely the promise held out for photography for many, many decades, perhaps 130 years if we count up through the late 1970s. And that is when I started taking pictures, at the very moment when the truth claims of the photograph were being dismantled by theory. That moment of the "Discourse of Others" has passed or shifted, but it marked me, changed for good the way I work.

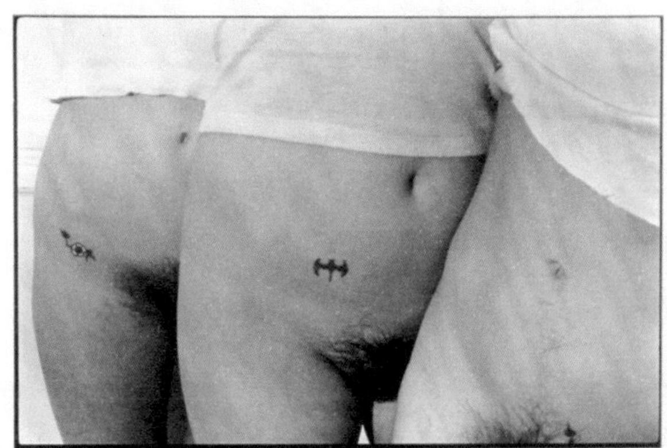

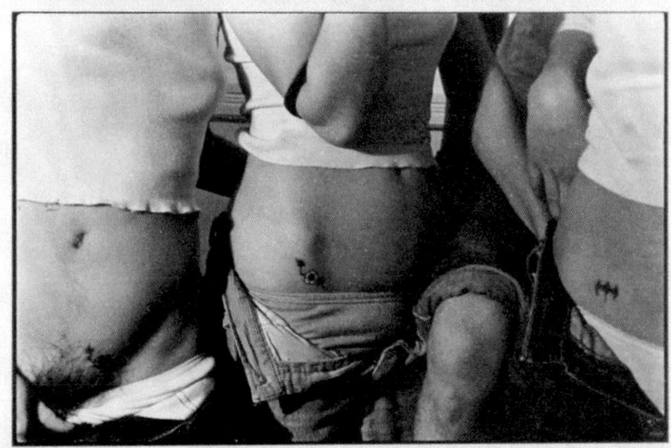

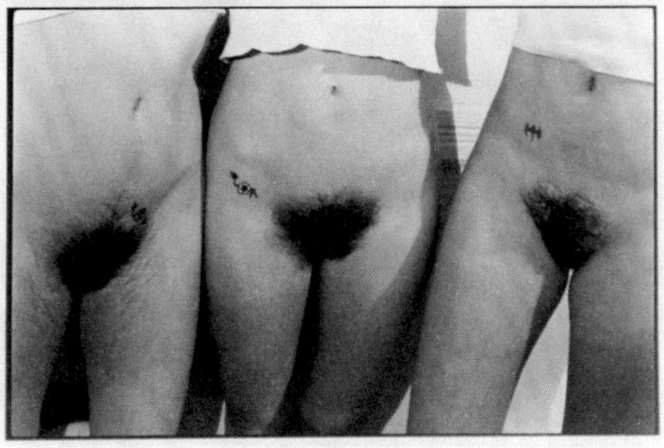

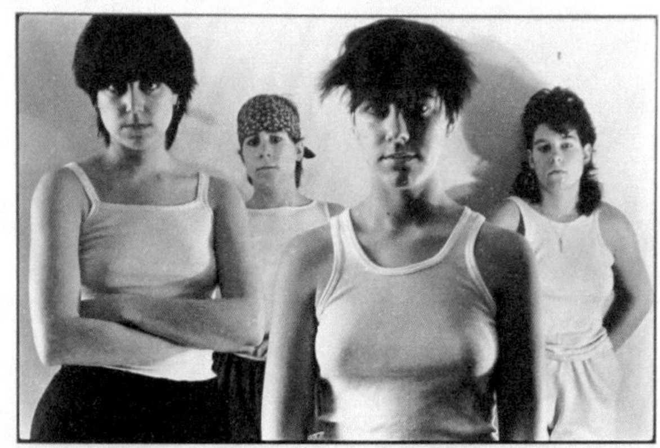

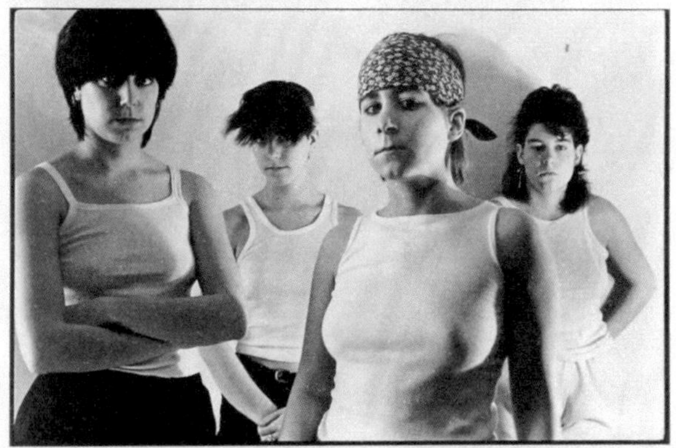

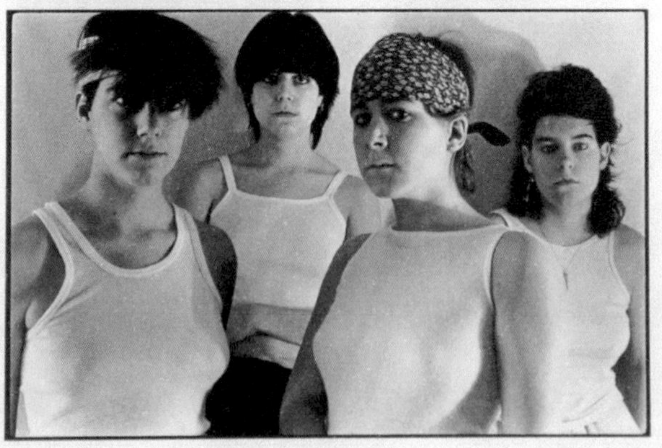

When I wrote about "being" four years ago, it was under the tapering effect of steroids. Now I take drugs that make me sleep. But this morning I woke early with precisely the idea of writing these lines and taking a picture of the rising sun reflected off the giant apartment building in the distance. Up at seven for the first time in . . . ? Photograph gleaming building—my old habit from when I'd wake with the sun.

* * *

CODA

On the subway downtown to the New York Public Library in search of Mary Shelley's diaries, I began to notice subway riders absorbed in writing of their own: a woman paying her bills, another marking pages on which the word *draft* is stamped in large letters. Some are standing, precariously balancing pads and pens on crowded trains; others look off into space, lost in concentration. There is a man folded over his crossword, whom I captured in the same pose on more than one day, and children doing their homework. A woman wearing orange velvet gloves clutches a small yellow pencil.

Just when I'd been writing about the disappearance of the figure from my photographs, I found myself taking street pictures again in the dim green light of the Manhattan subway. I experienced the same unease and doubt I've always had in taking pictures on the street, and I kept expecting to be asked what I was doing. But the writers themselves, eyes downcast, were unaware of my camera, and those looking on, over my own shoulder even, seem only mildly surprised by the small point-and-shoot, a note-taker itself, recording the underground writers as we ride.

2011

LES GODDESSES

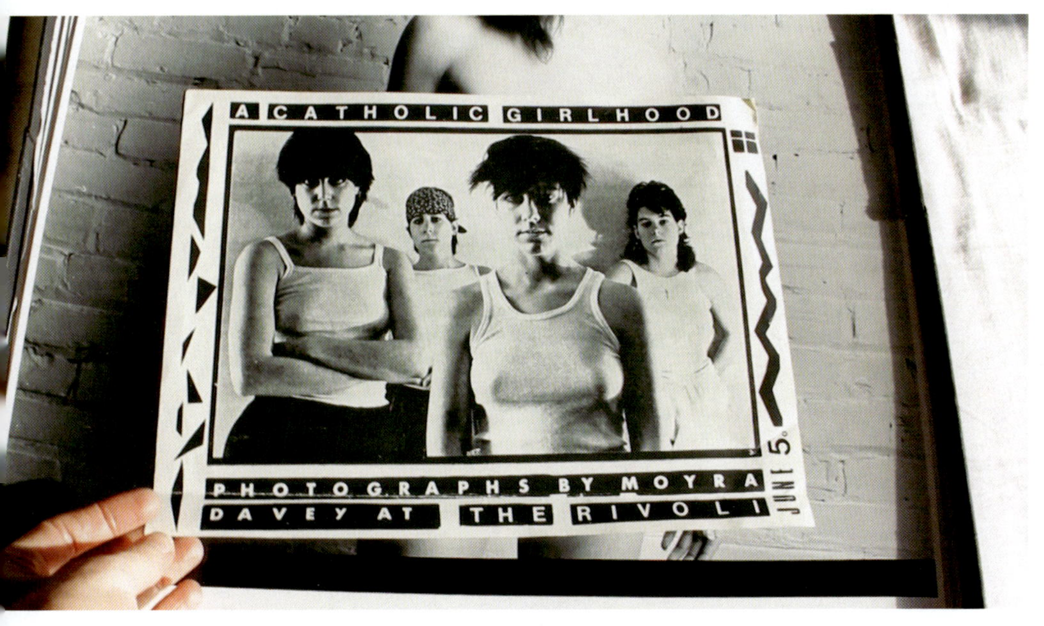

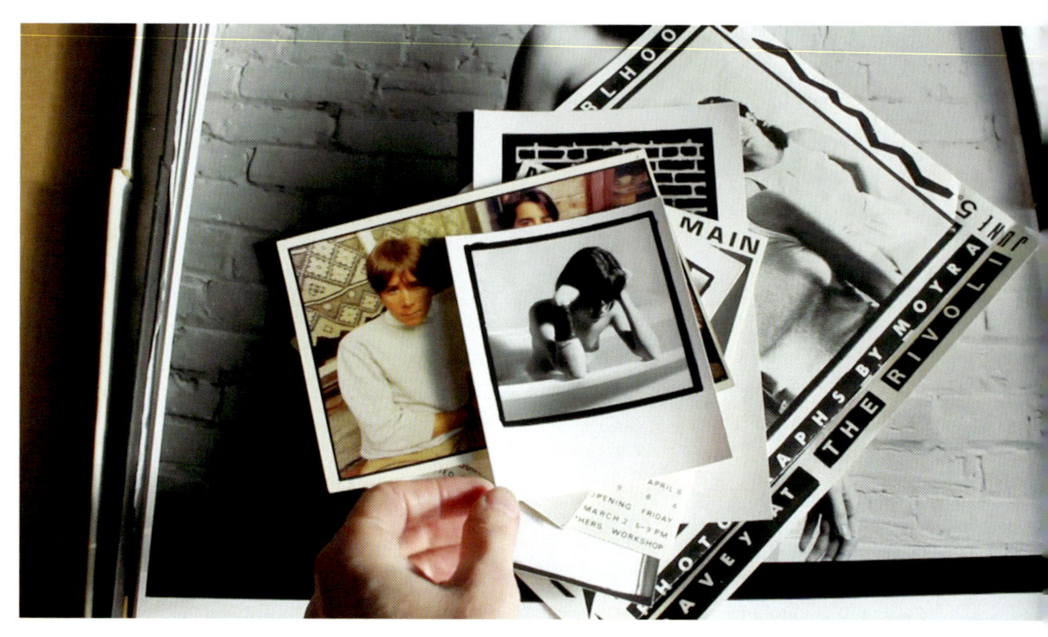
MAIN
JUNE 5
APHS BY MOYRA
THE RIVOLI
APRIL 8
OPENING FRIDAY
MARCH 2 5–9 PM
WORKSHOP

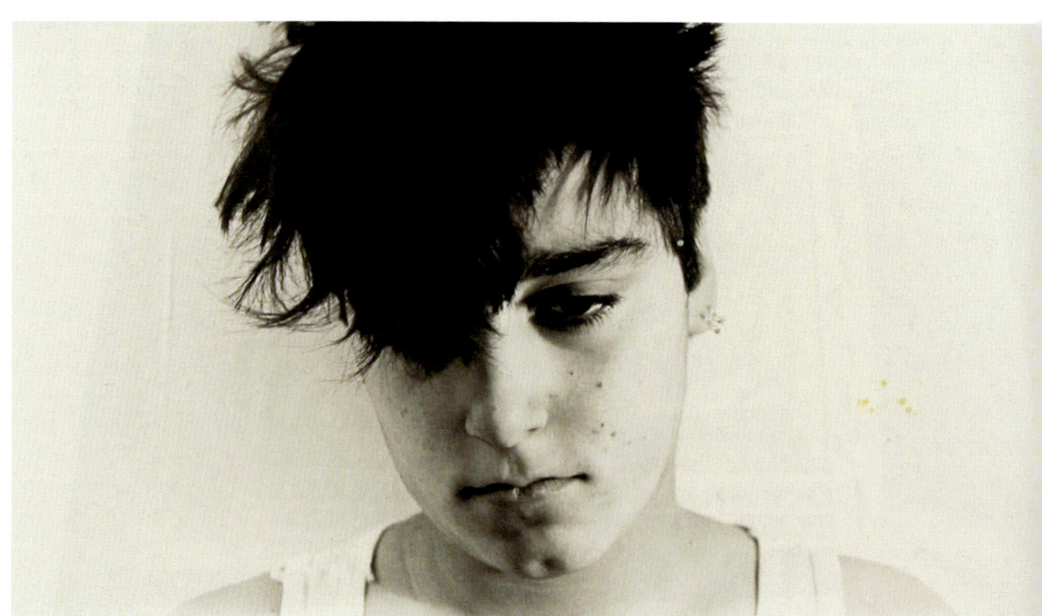

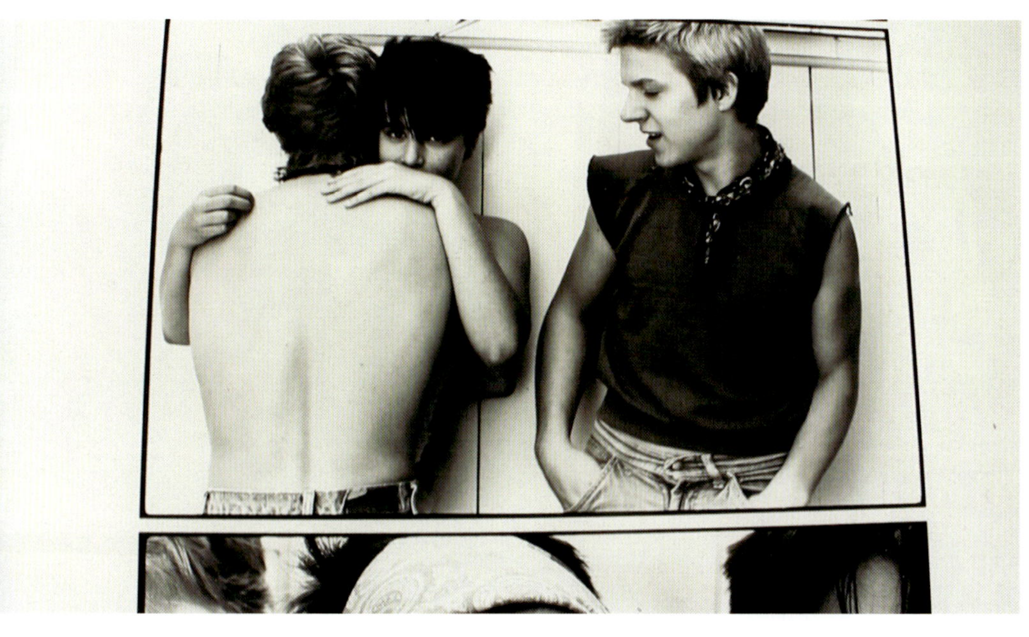

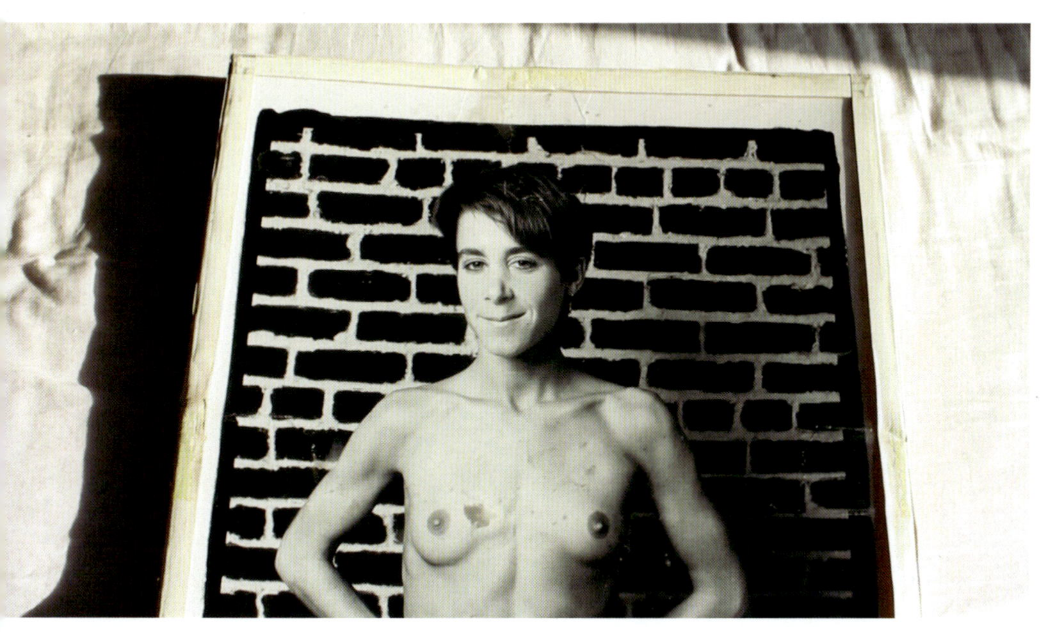

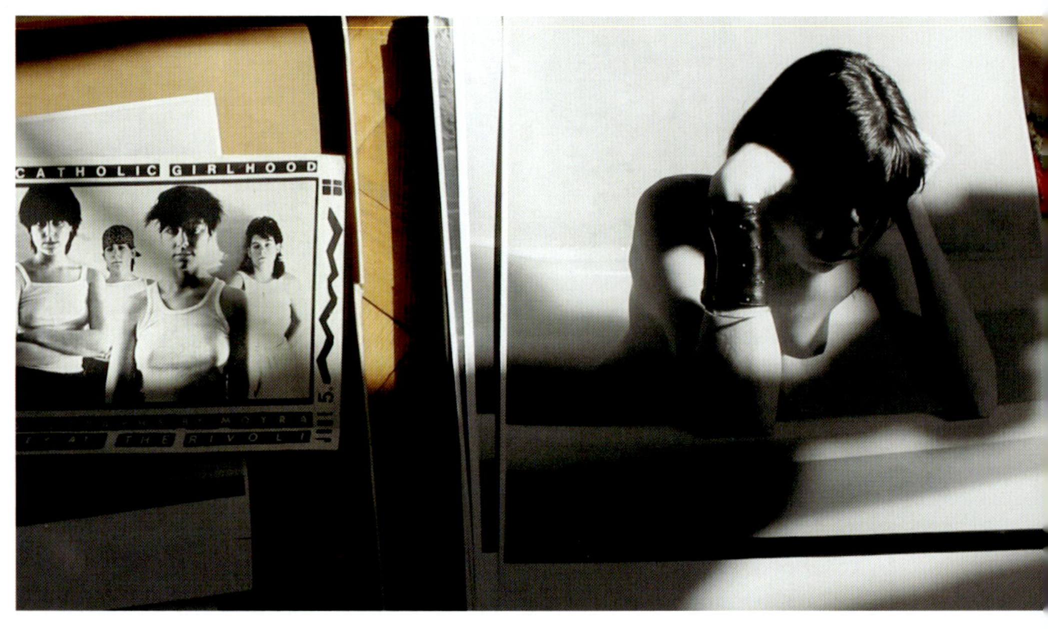
CATHOLIC GIRLHOOD
MOYRA
THE RIVOLI
JUNE 5.

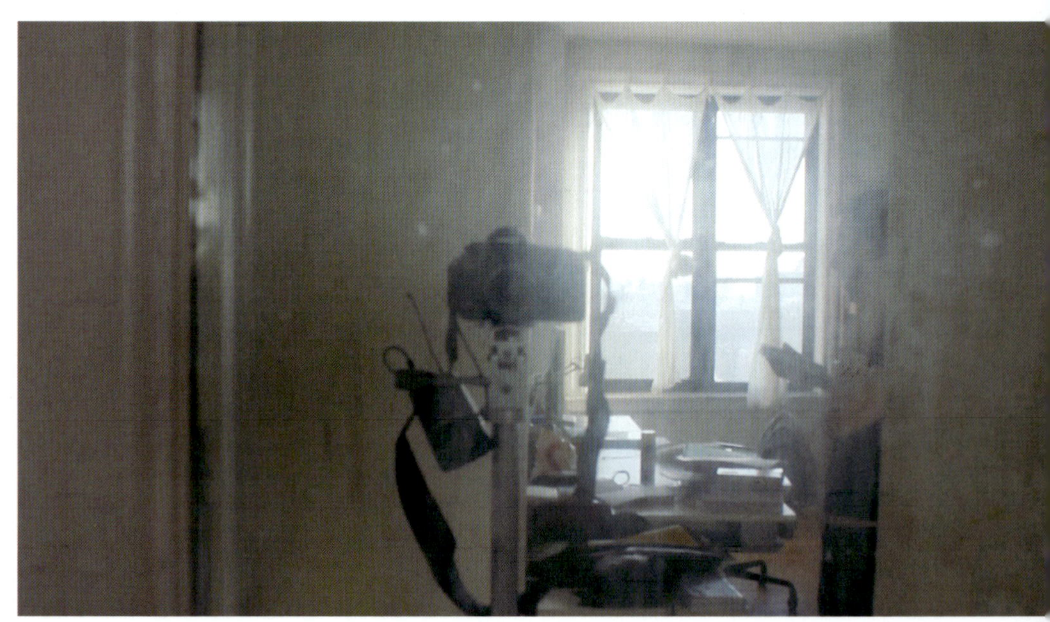

HISTORY

OF

A SIX WEEKS TOUR

THROUGH

A PART OF FRANCE,
SWITZERLAND, GERMANY, AND HOLLAND

WITH LETTERS

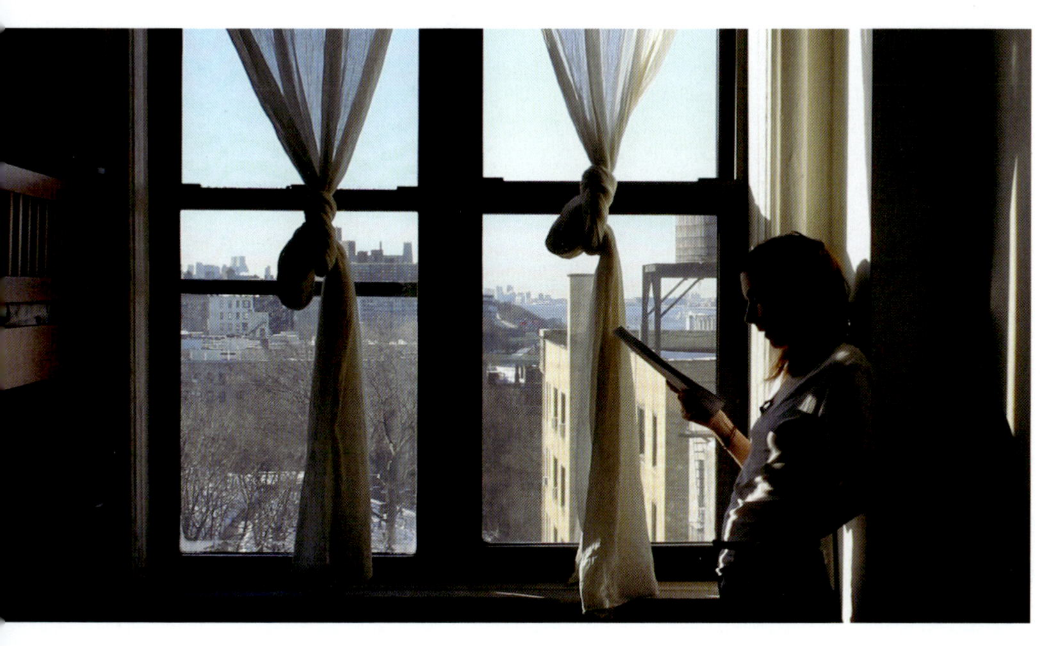

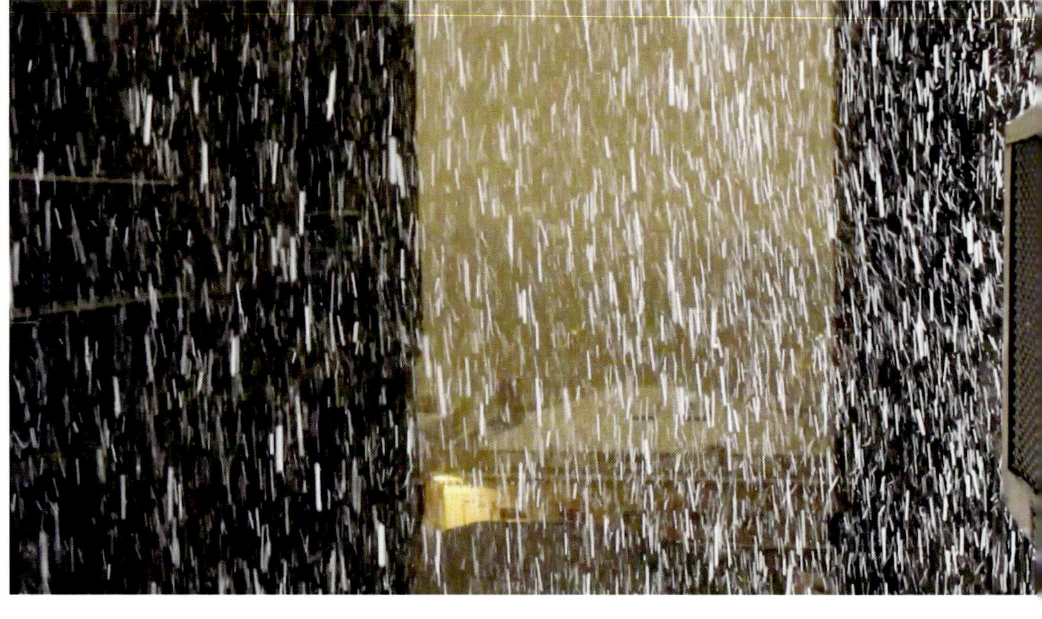

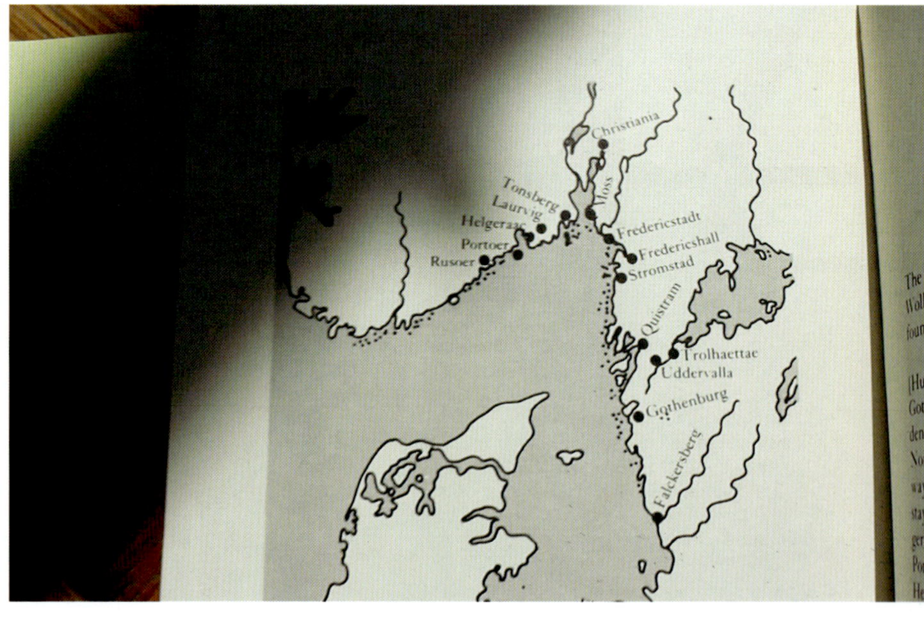
Christiania
Tonsberg
Laurvig
Moss
Helgeraac
Portoer
Rusoer
Fredericstadt
Fredericshall
Stromstad
Quistram
Trolhaettae
Uddervalla
Gothenburg
Falckersberg

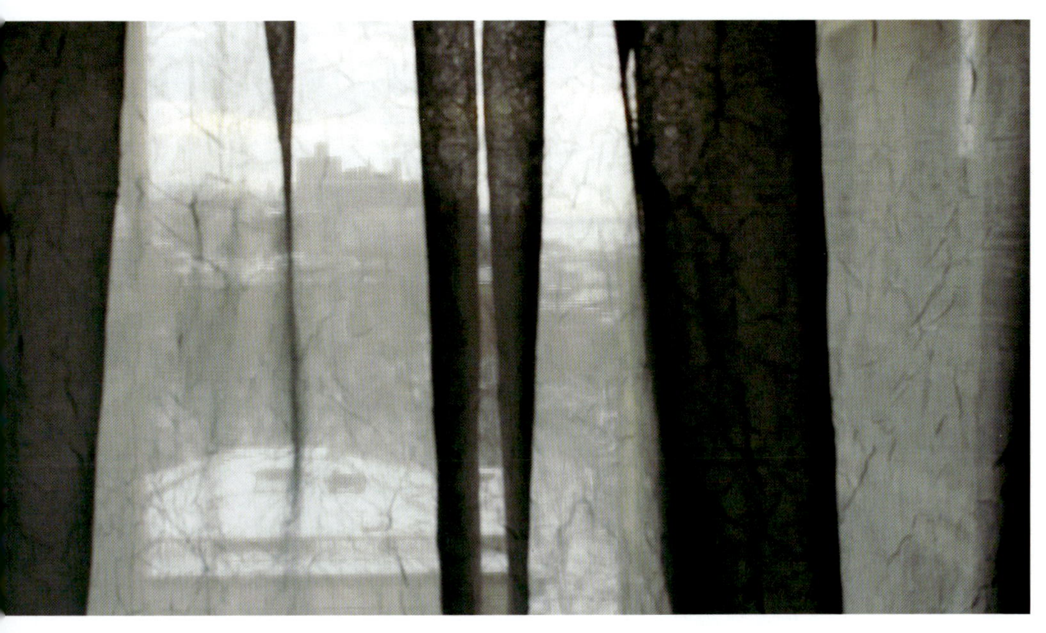

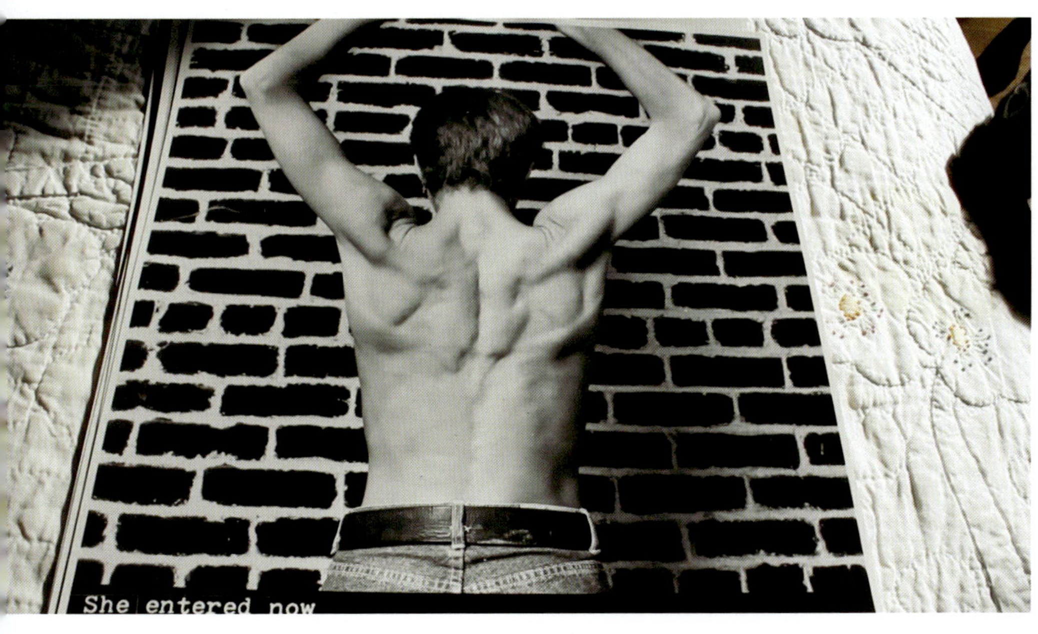
She entered now

NOTHING can be more unpresuming than this little volume. It contains the account of some desultory visits by a party of young people to scenes which are now so familiar to our countrymen, that few facts relating to them can be expected to have escaped the

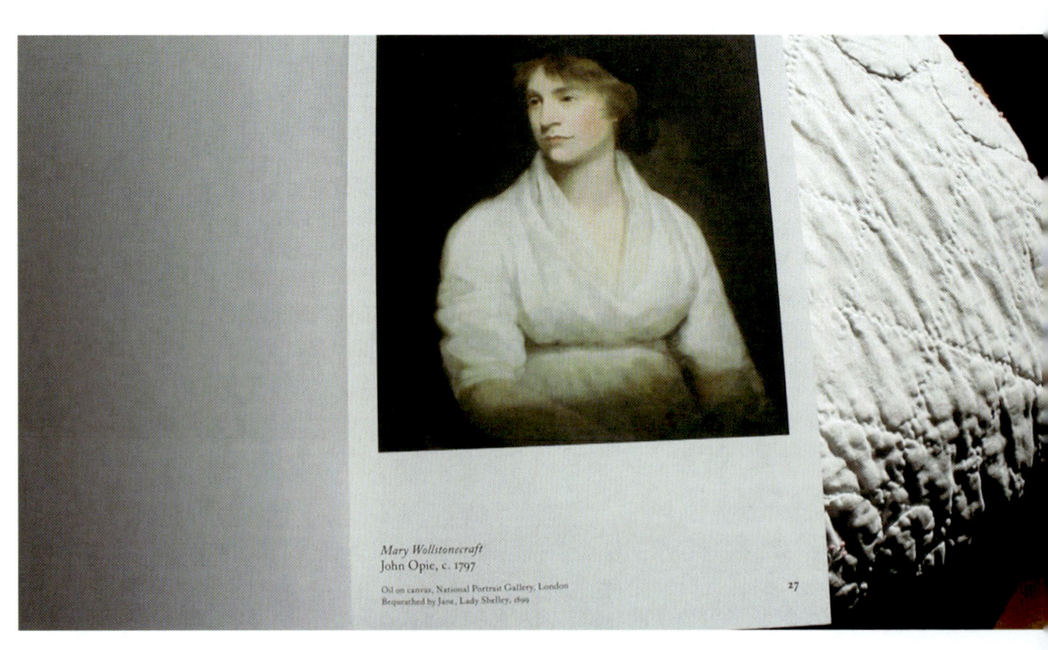

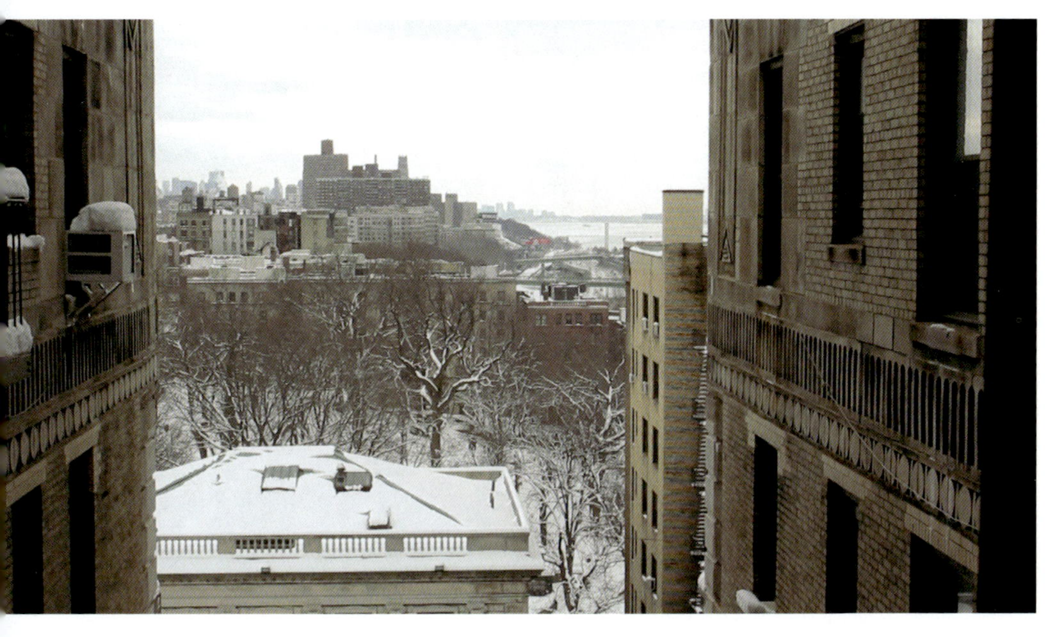

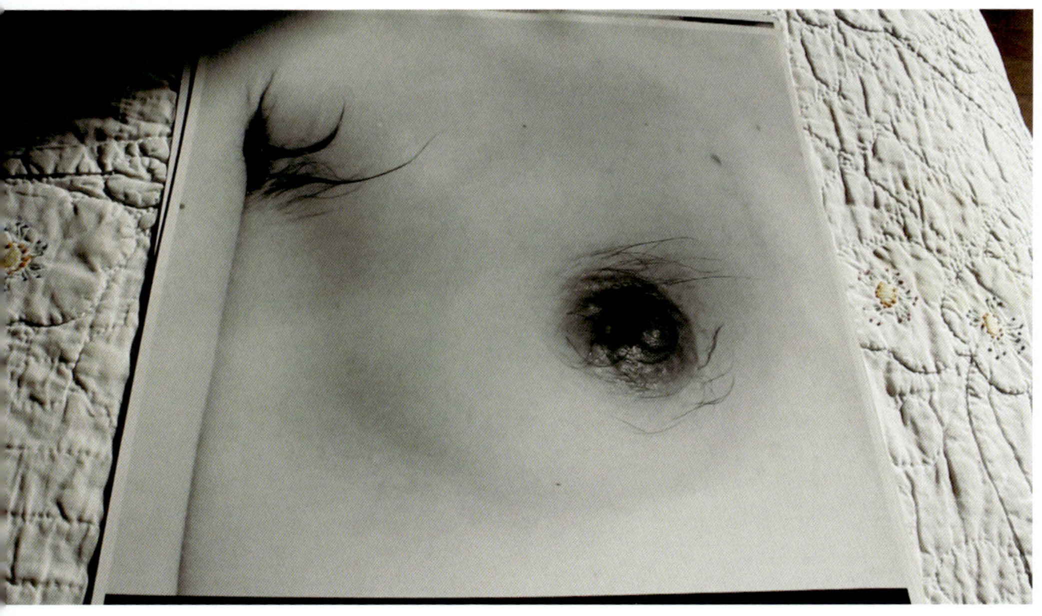

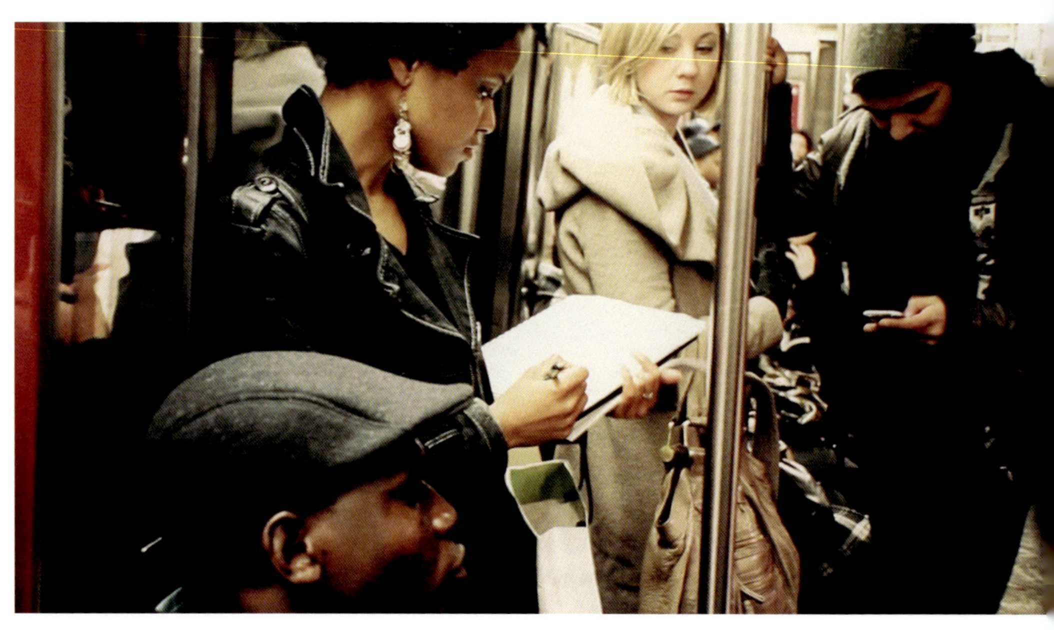

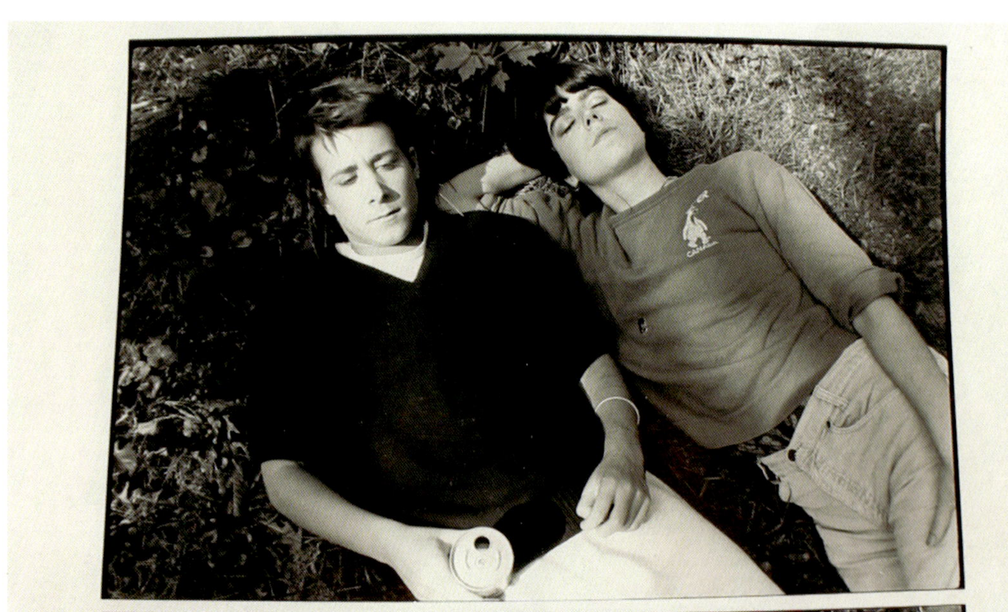

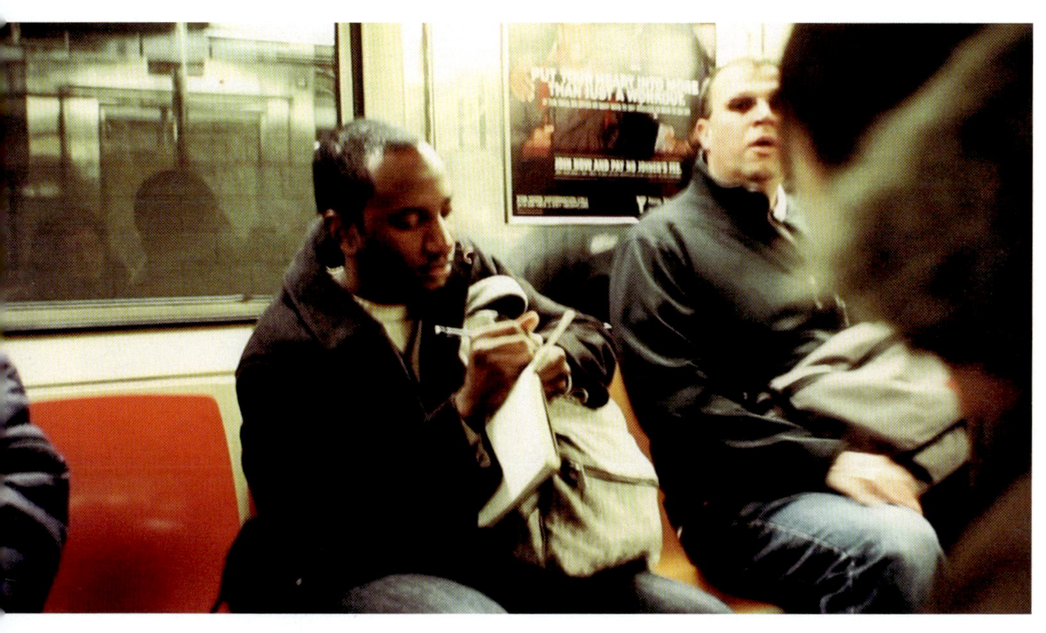
PUT YOUR HEART INTO MORE THAN JUST A WORKOUT.
JOIN NOW AND PAY NO JOINER'S FEE.

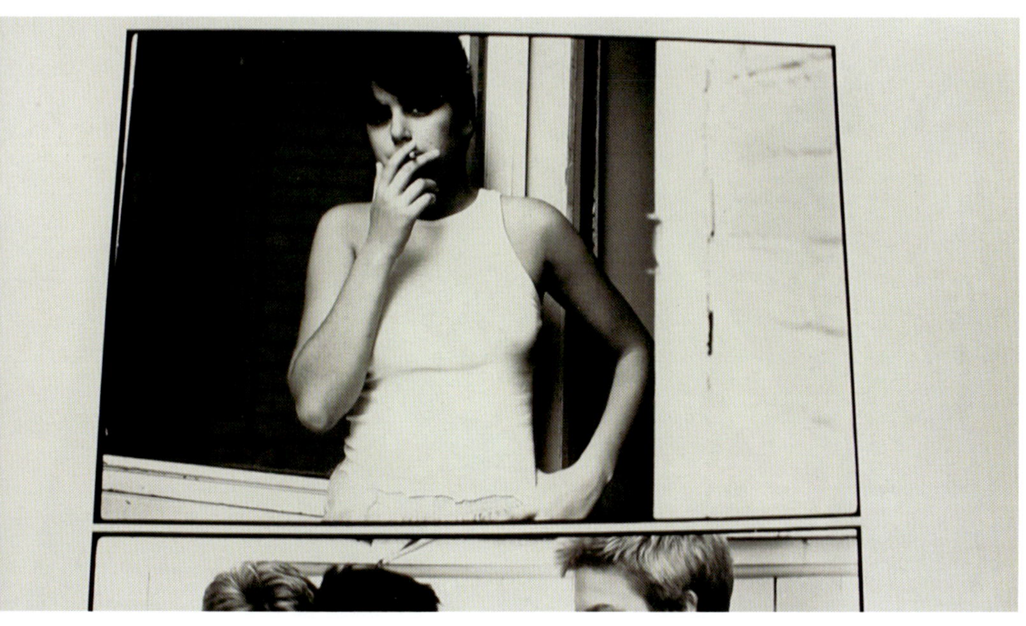

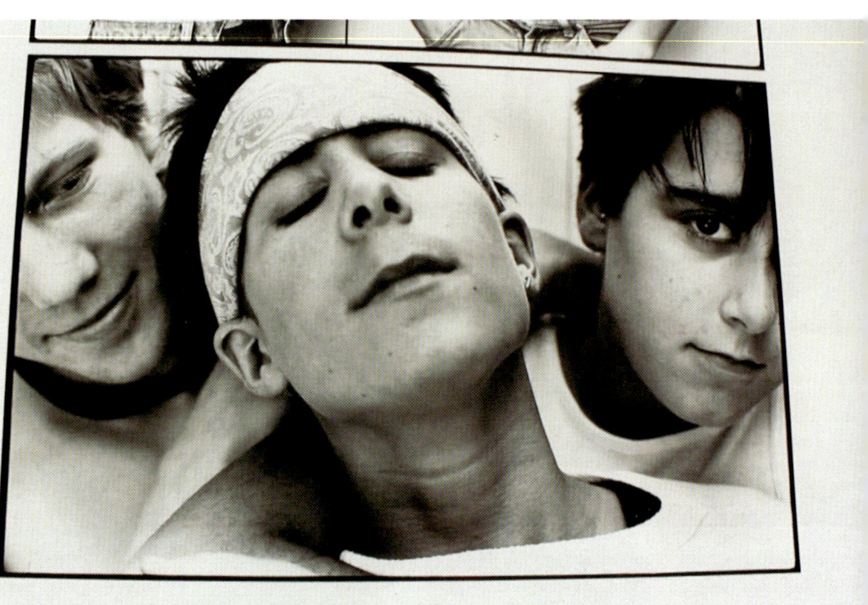

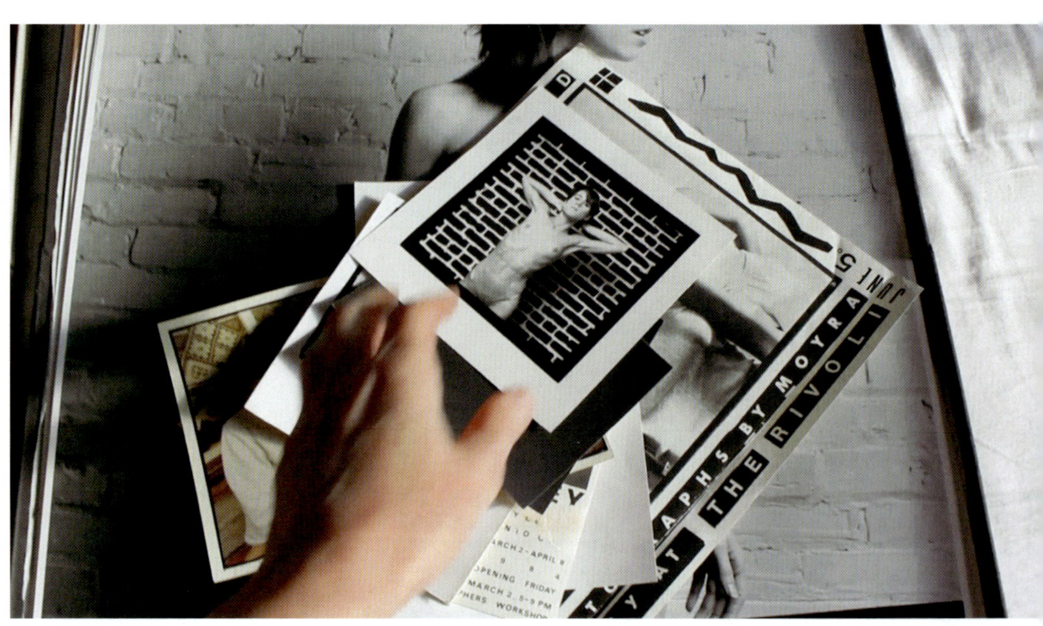
JUNE 5
APHS BY MOYRA
AT THE RIVOLI
OPENING FRIDAY
MARCH 2, 5-9 PM
PHERS WORKSHOP

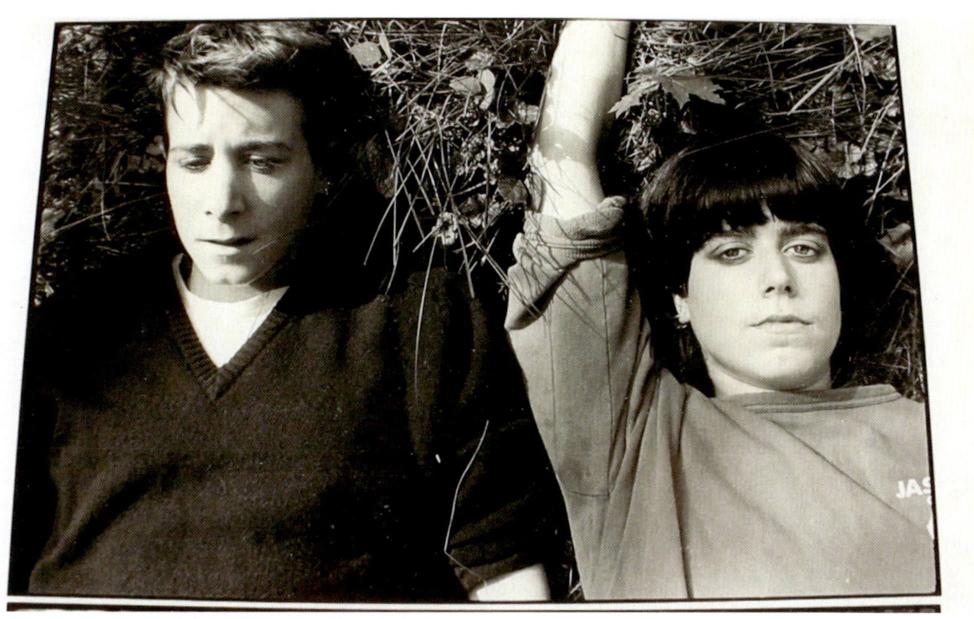

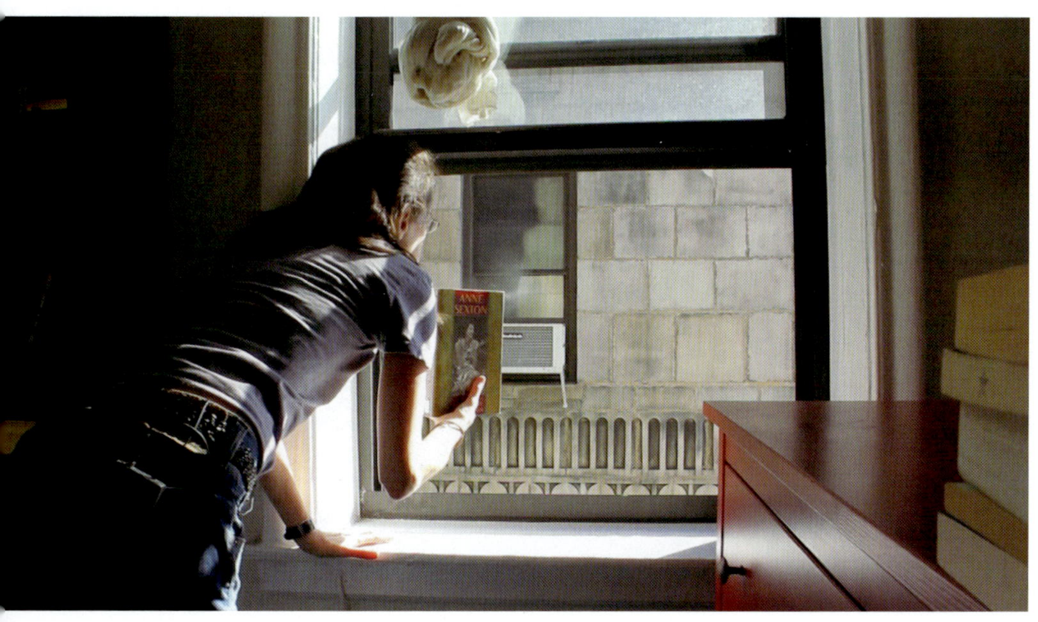
ANNE
SEXTON

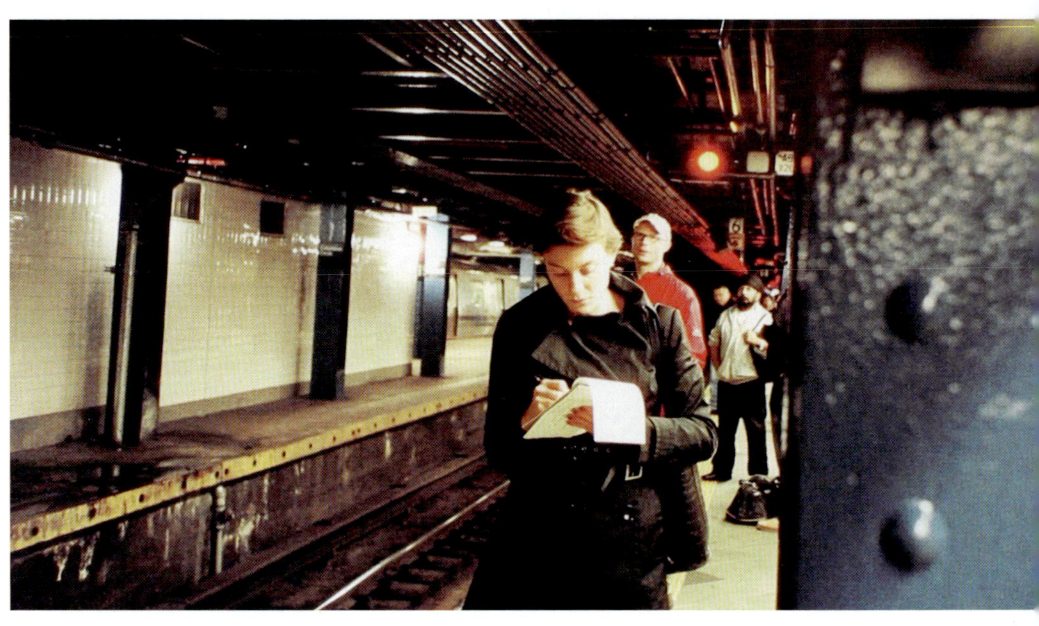

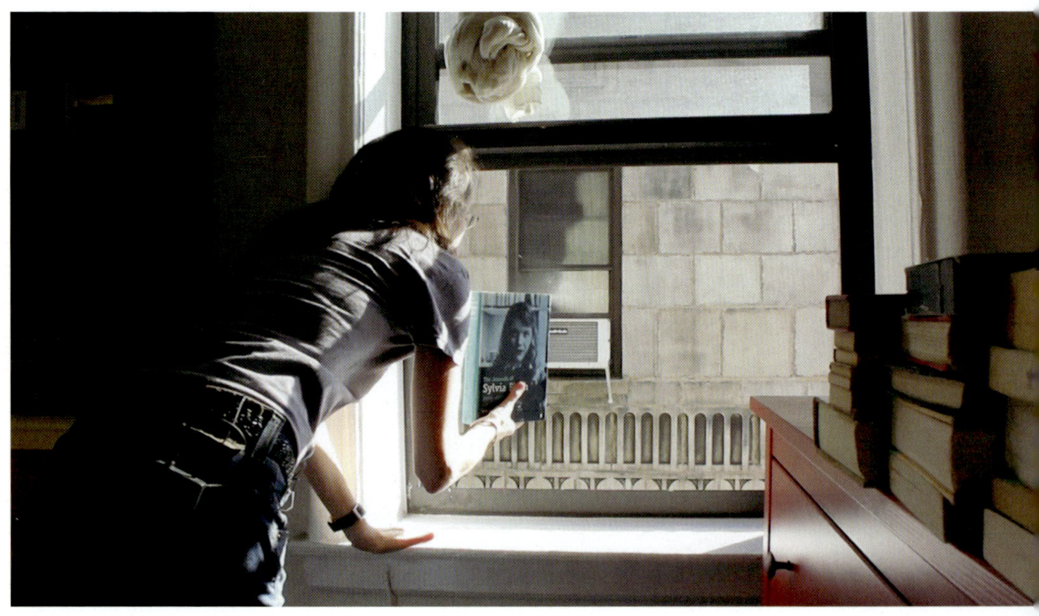
Sylvia

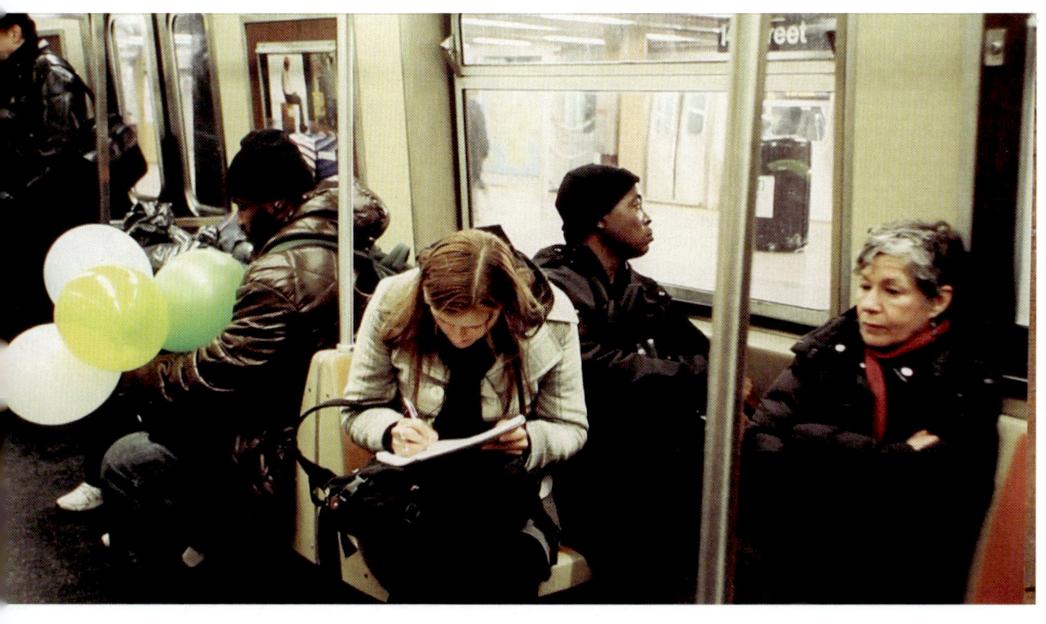

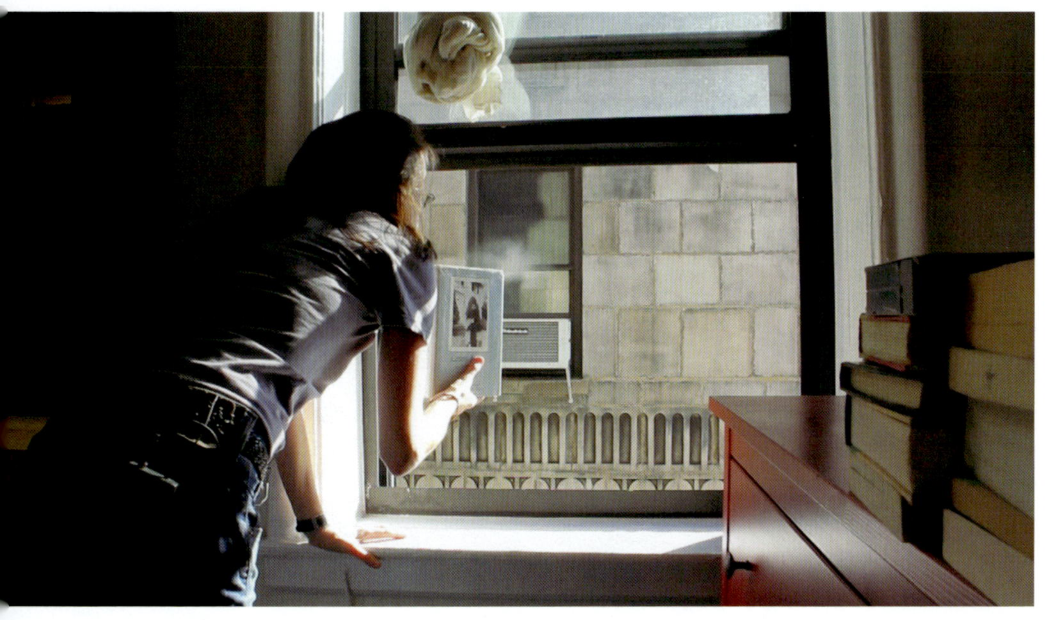

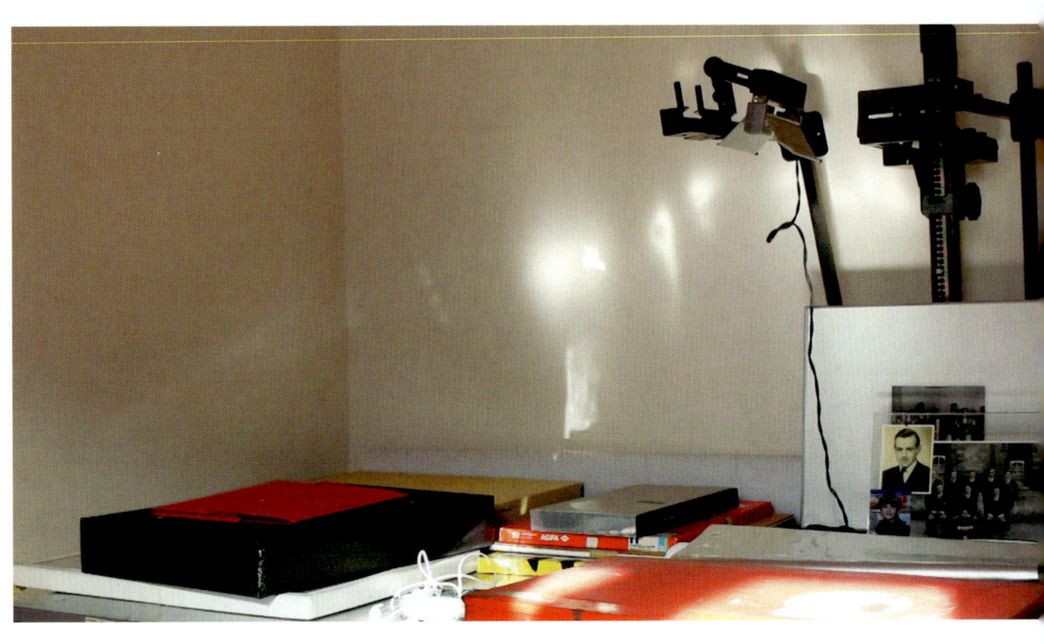
AGFA

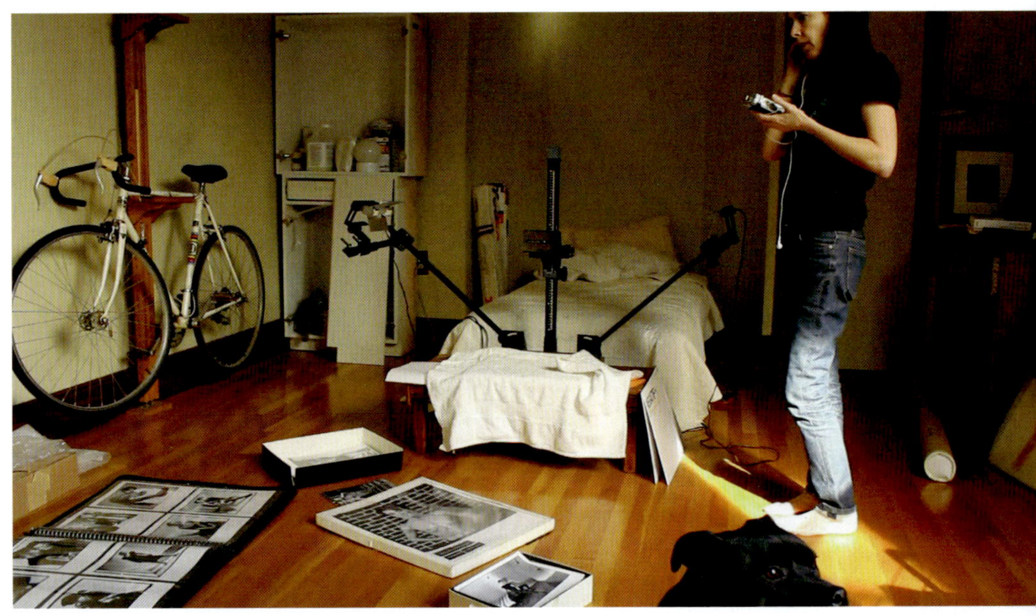

HEMLOCK FOREST

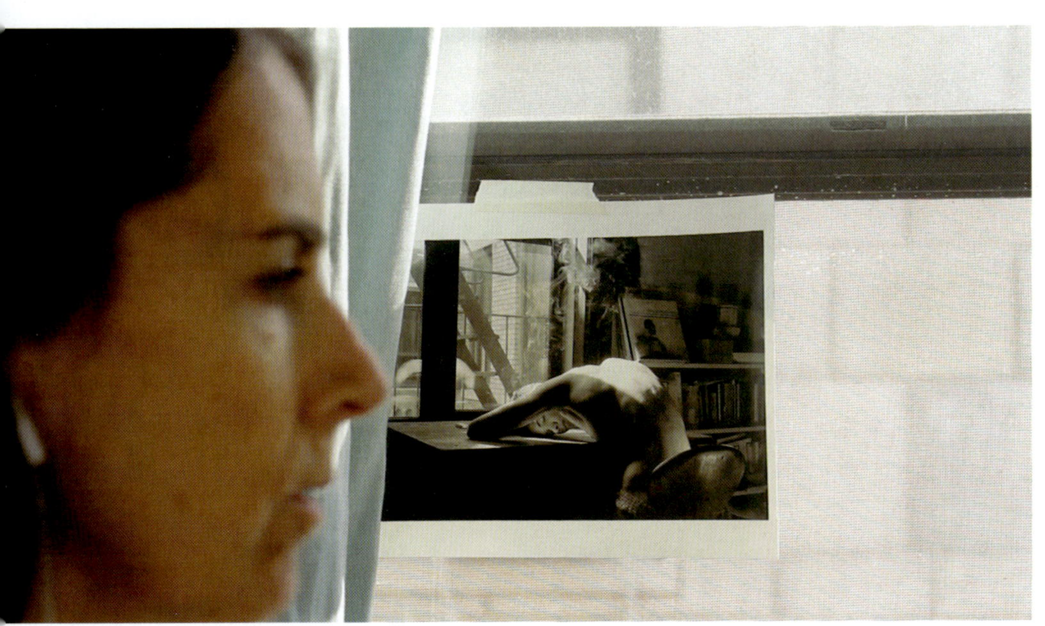

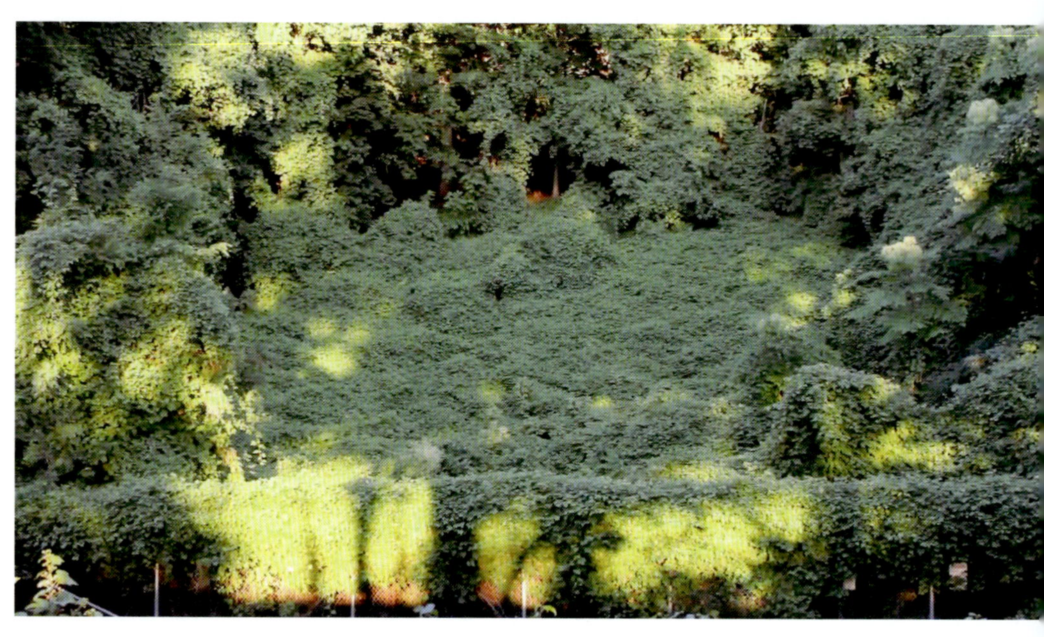

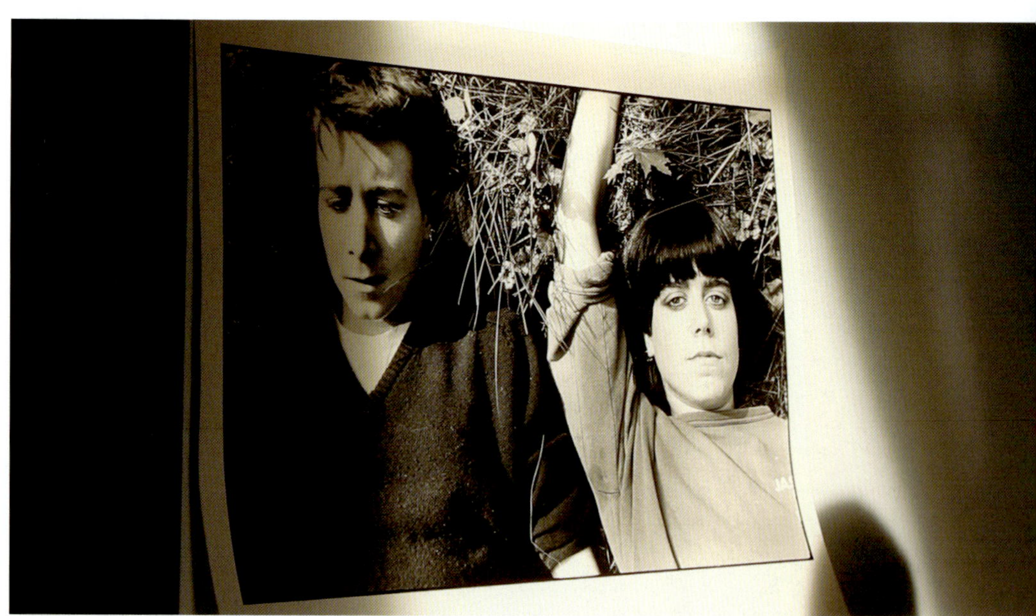

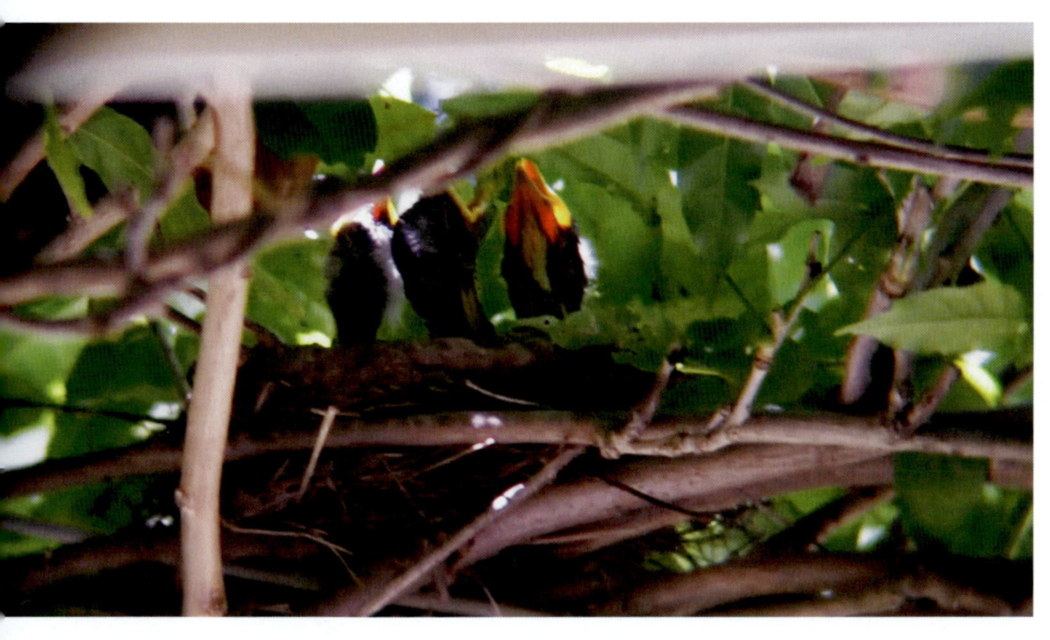

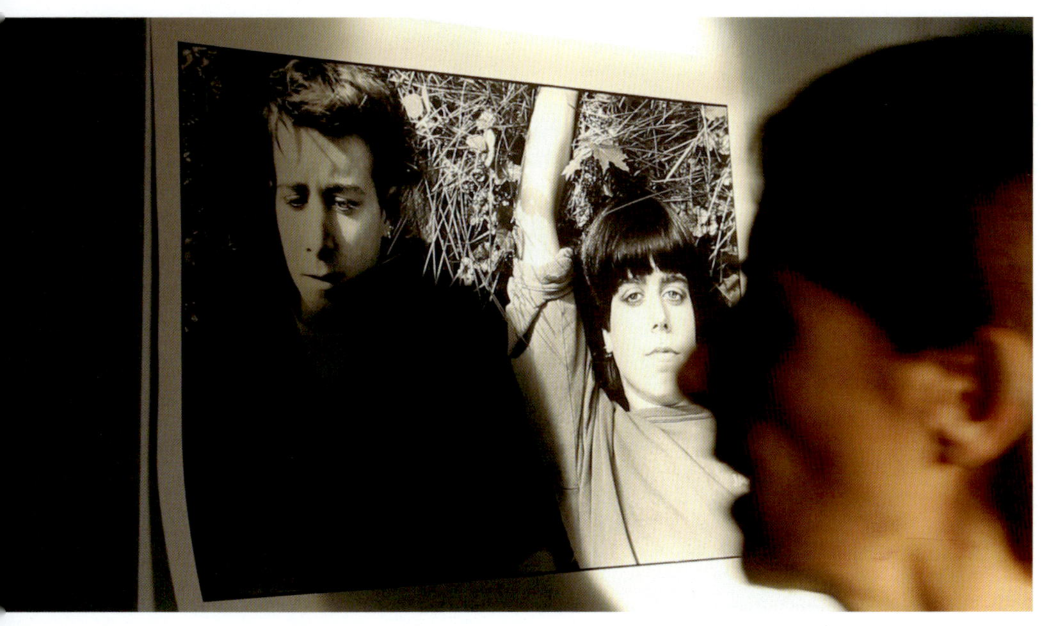

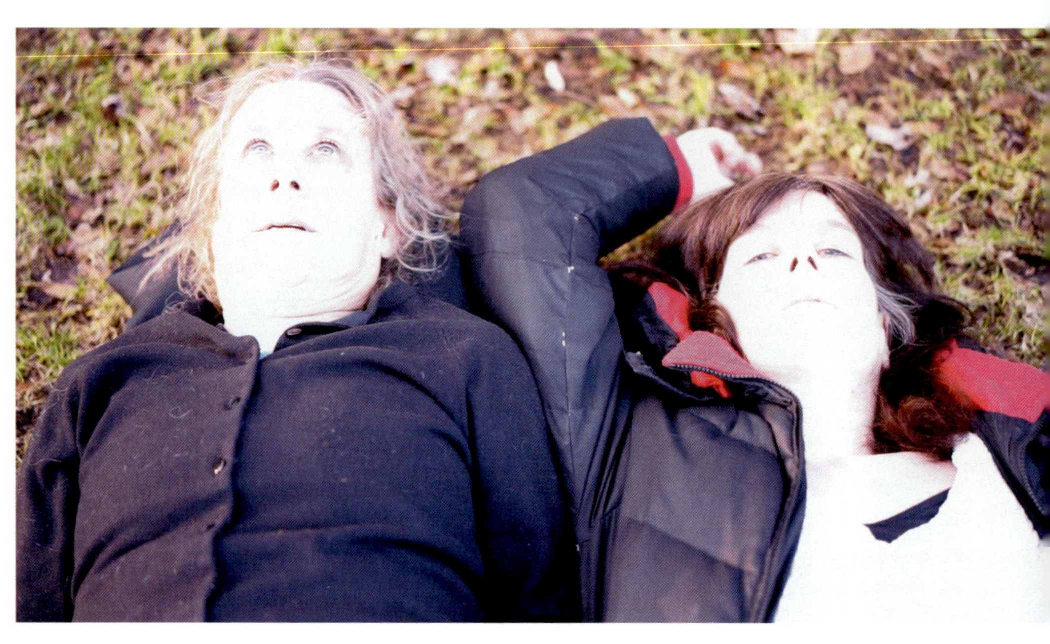

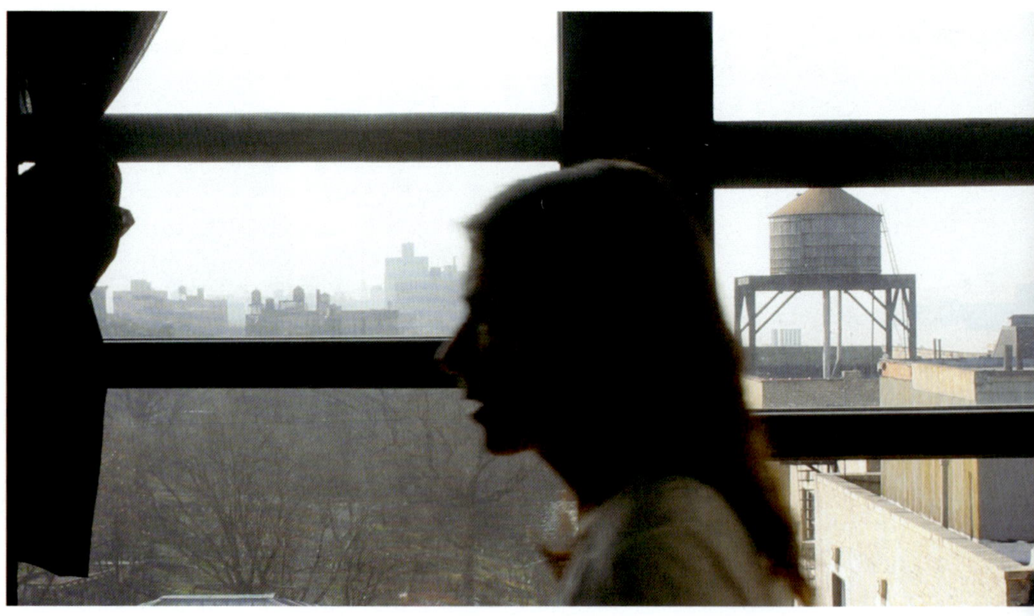

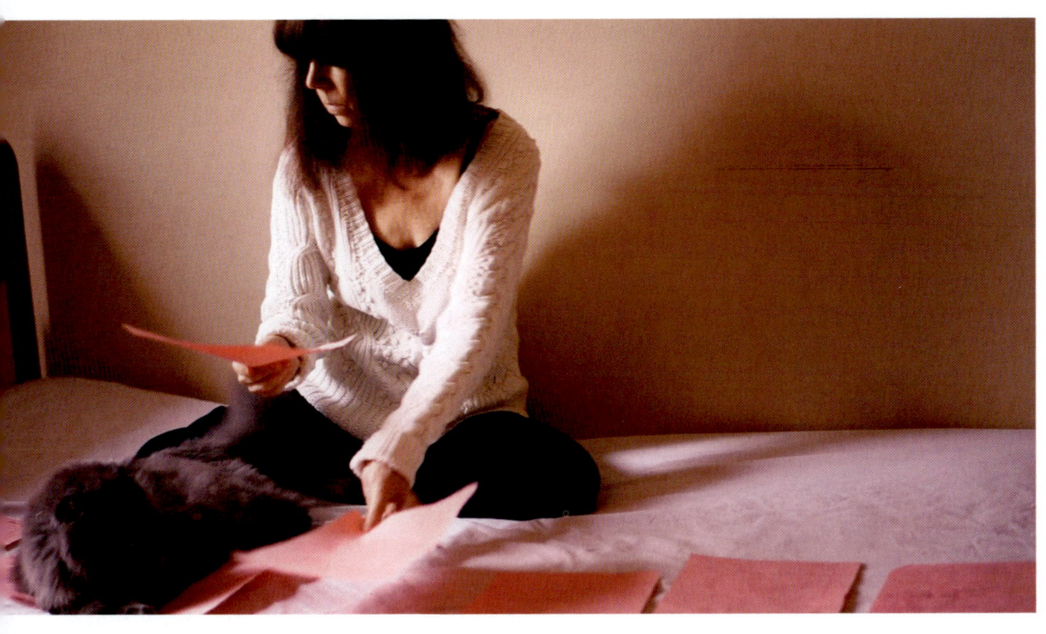

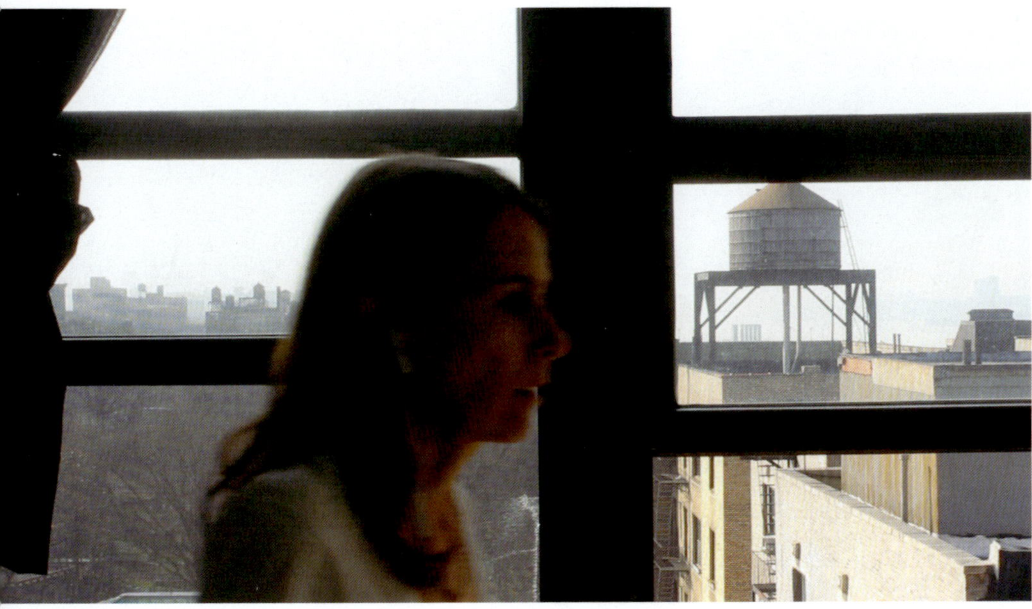

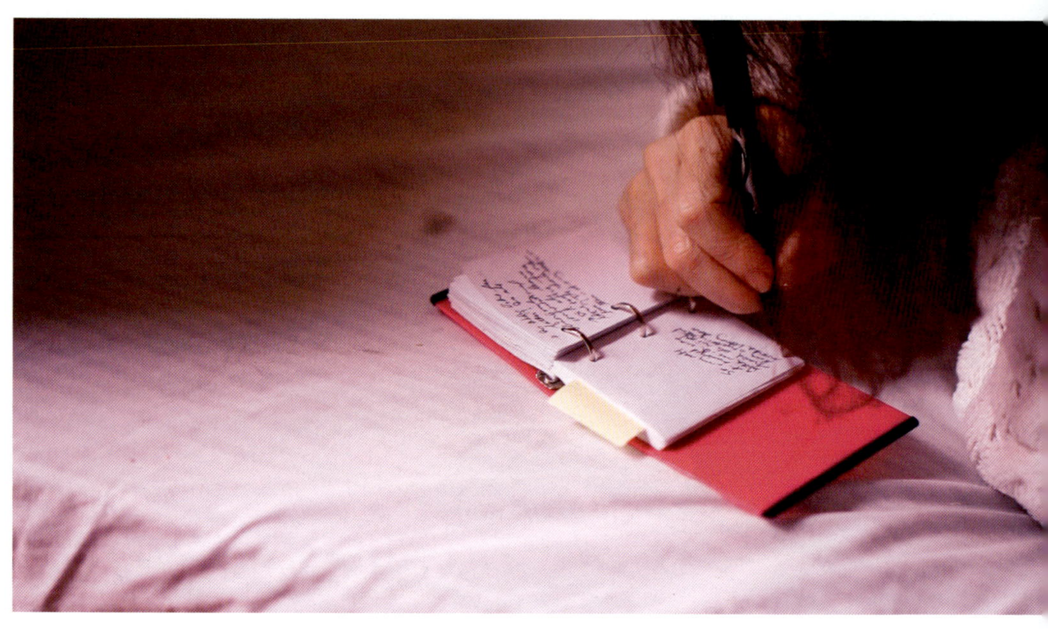

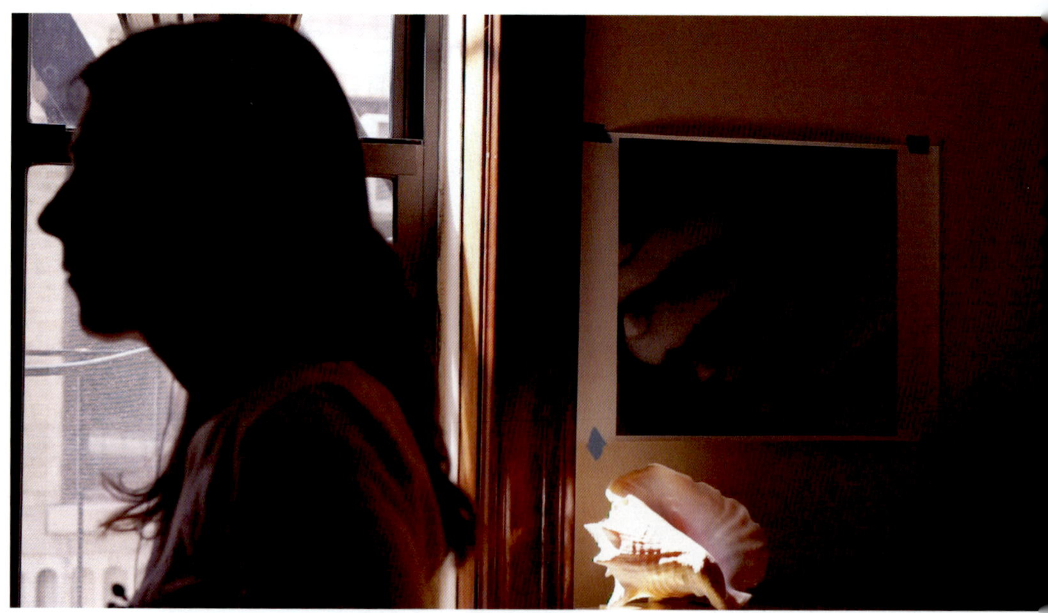

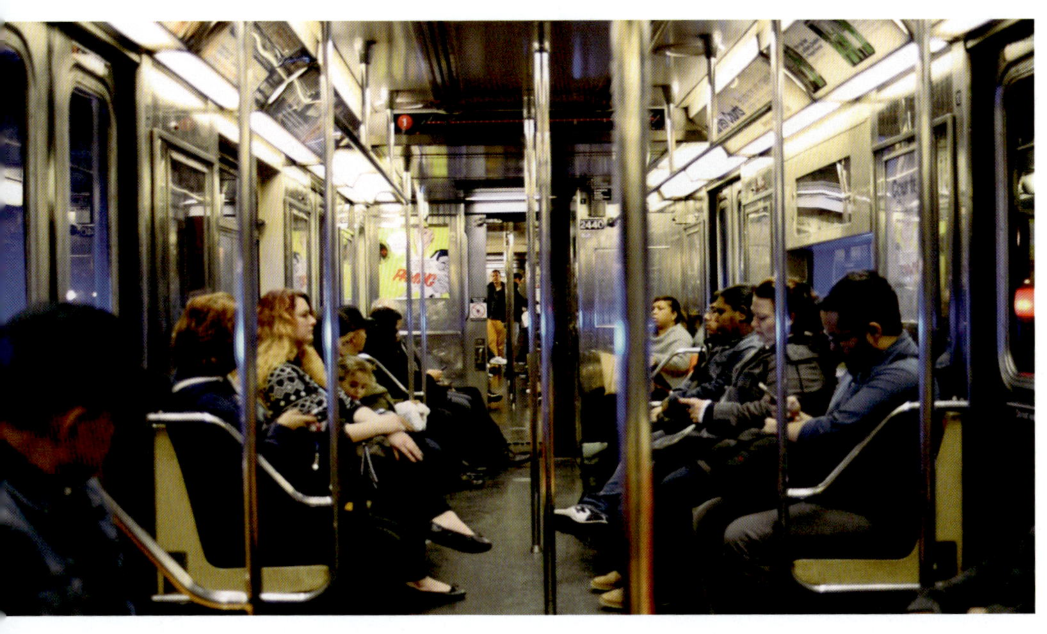

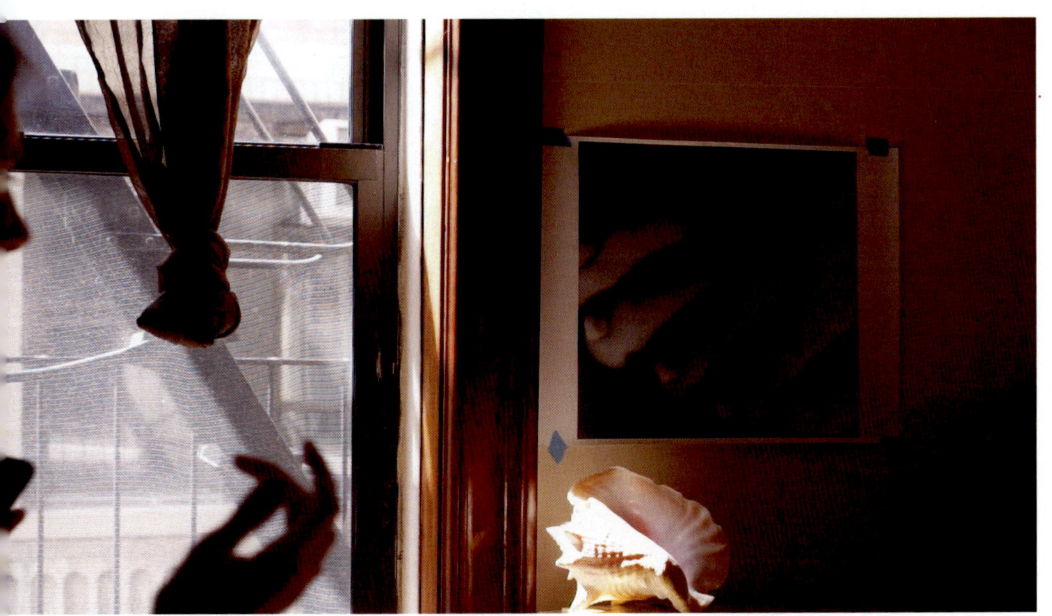

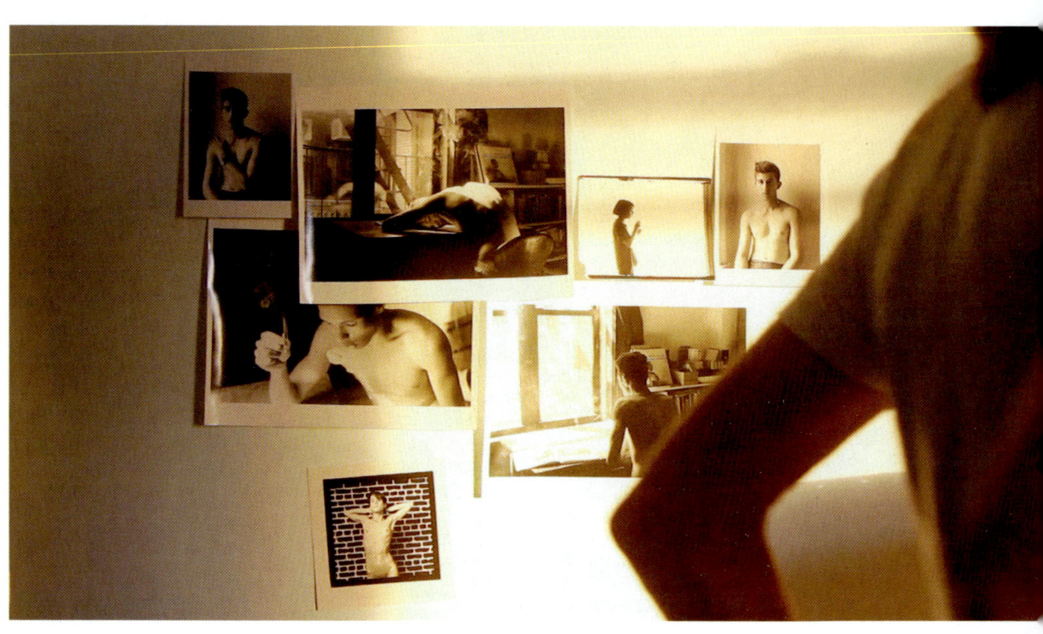

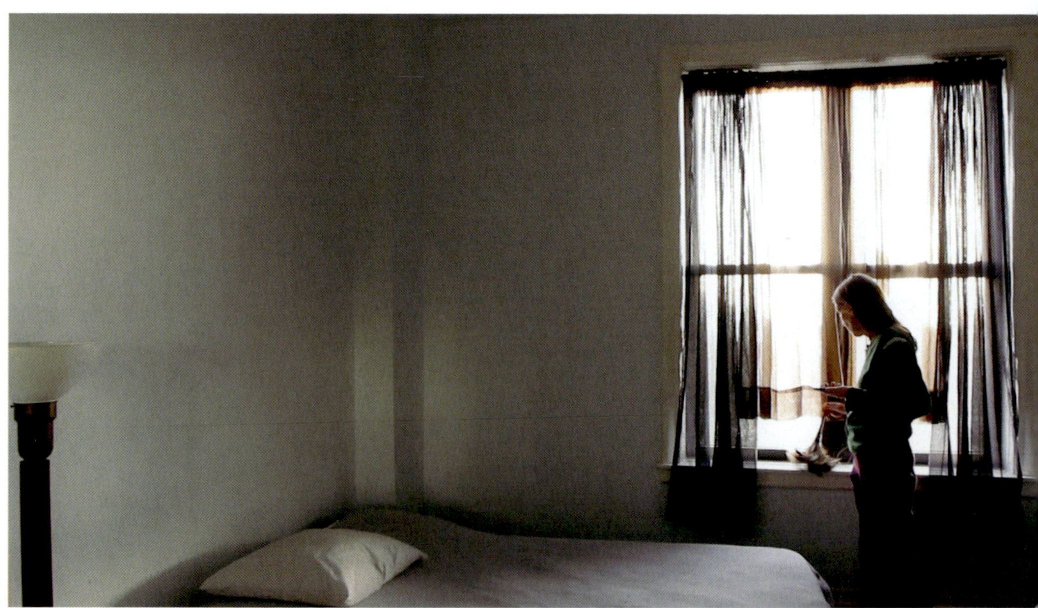

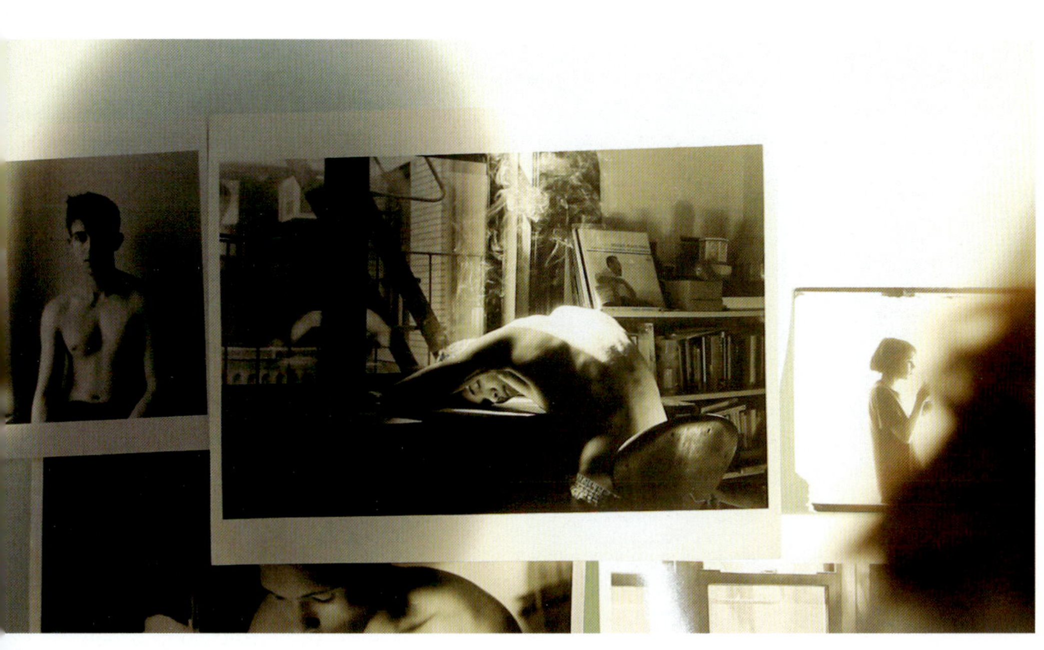

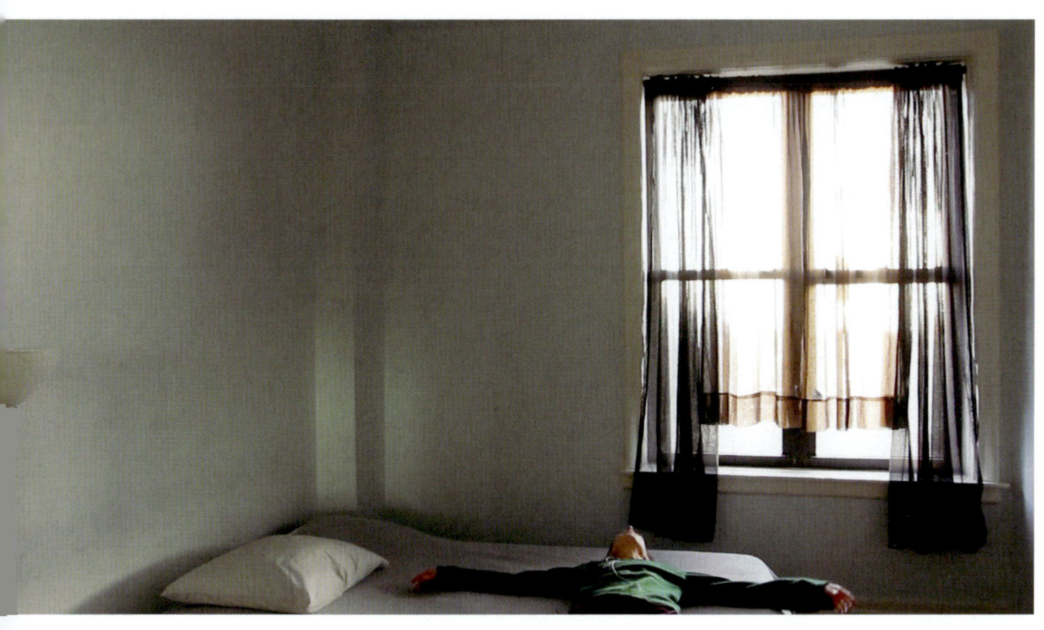

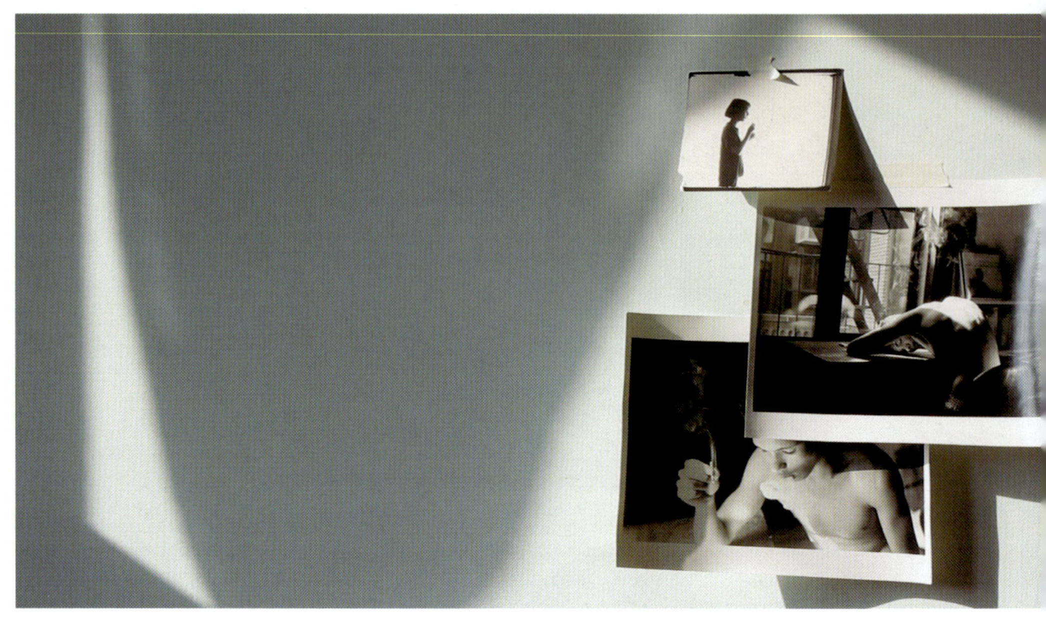

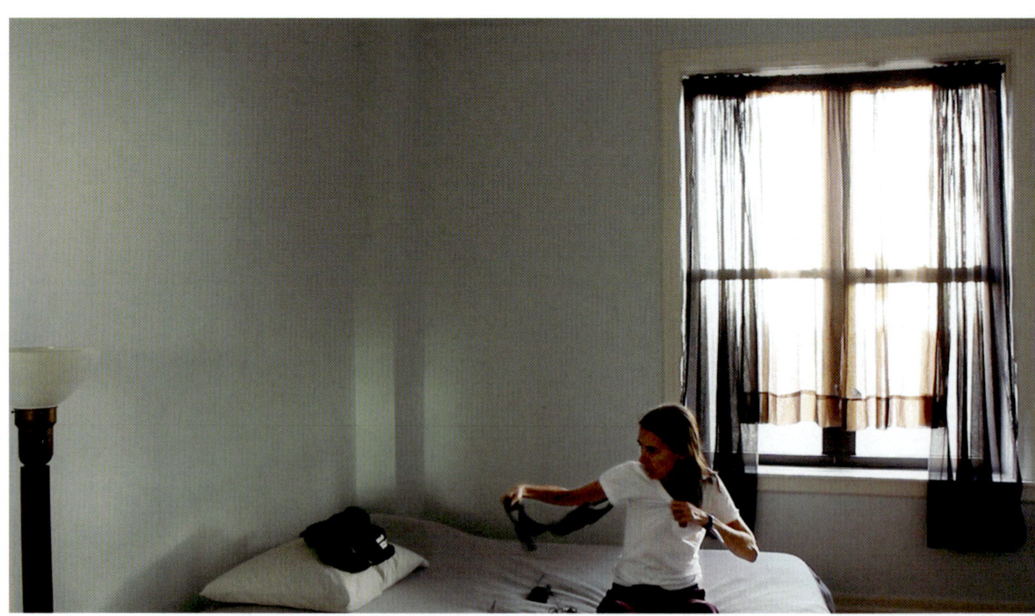

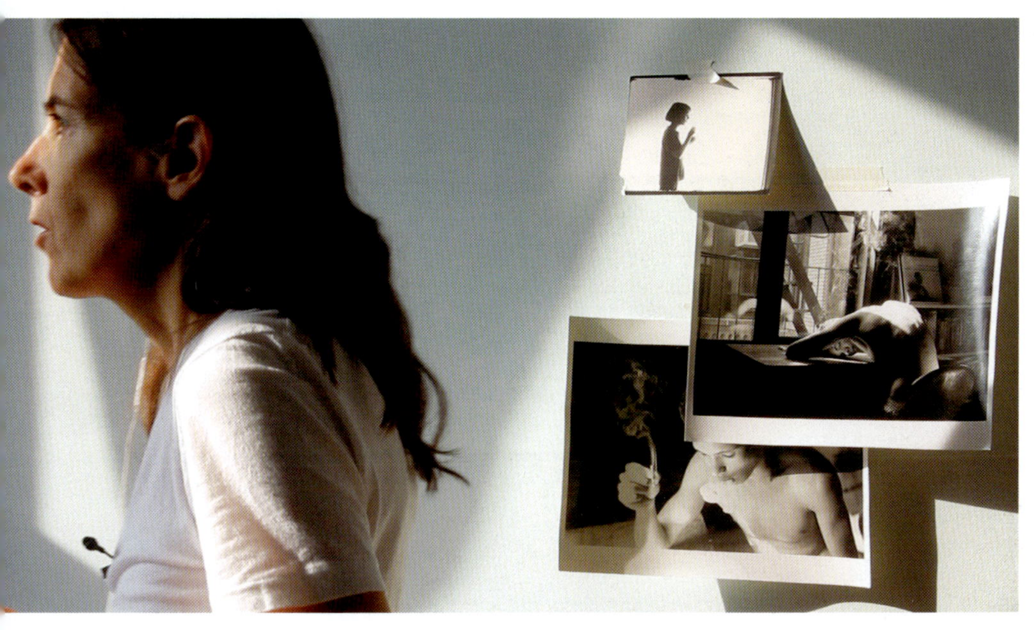

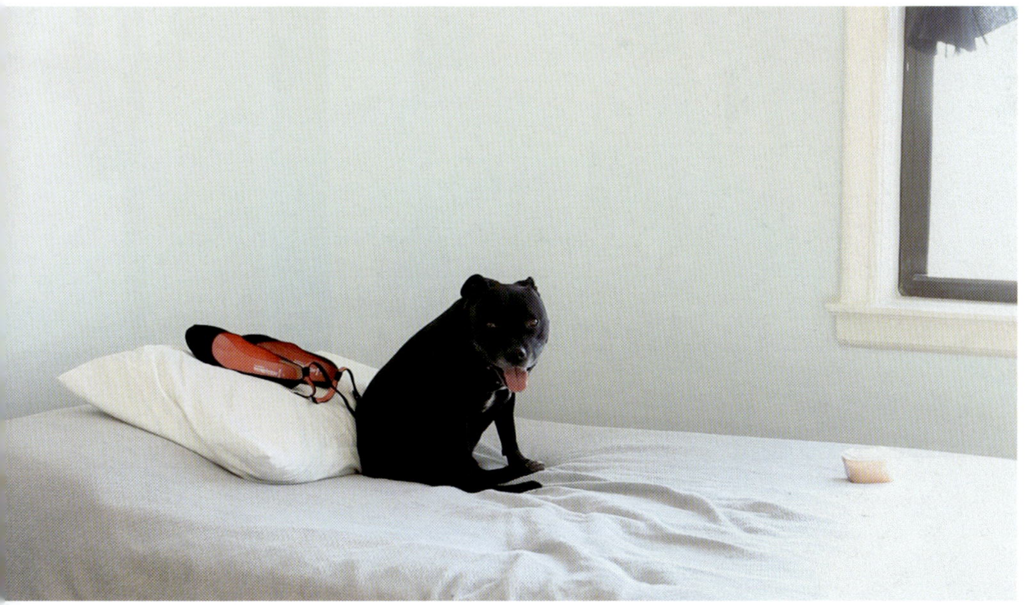

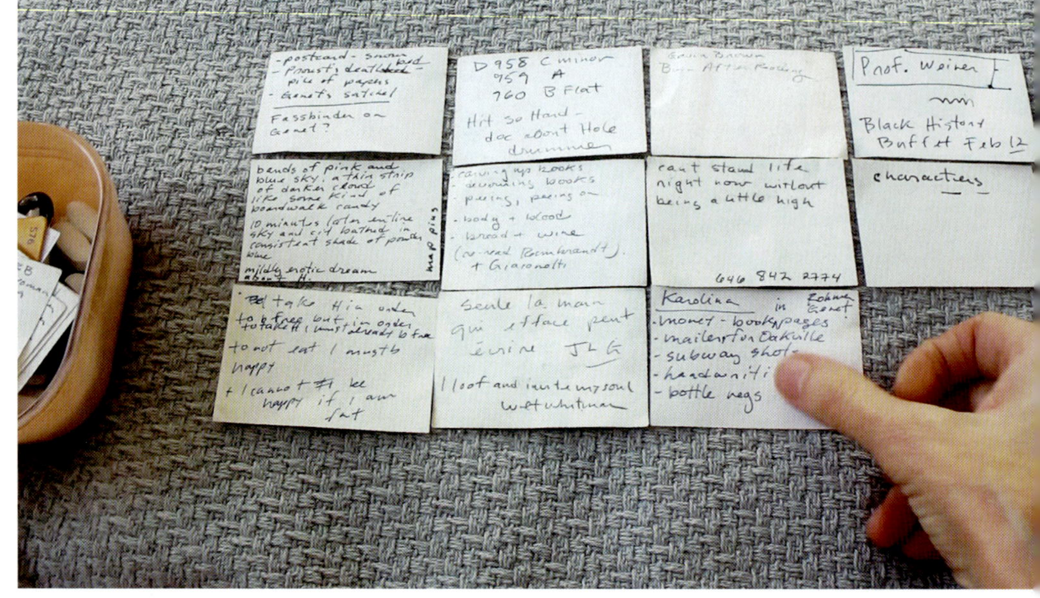

Fassbinder on Genet?
Hit So Hard -
doc about Hole
Prof. Weiner
Black History
Buffet Feb 12
characters
cant stand life
right now without
being a little high
646 842 2774
Seule la main
qui efface peut
écrire JLG
I loaf and invite my soul
walt whitman
Karolina

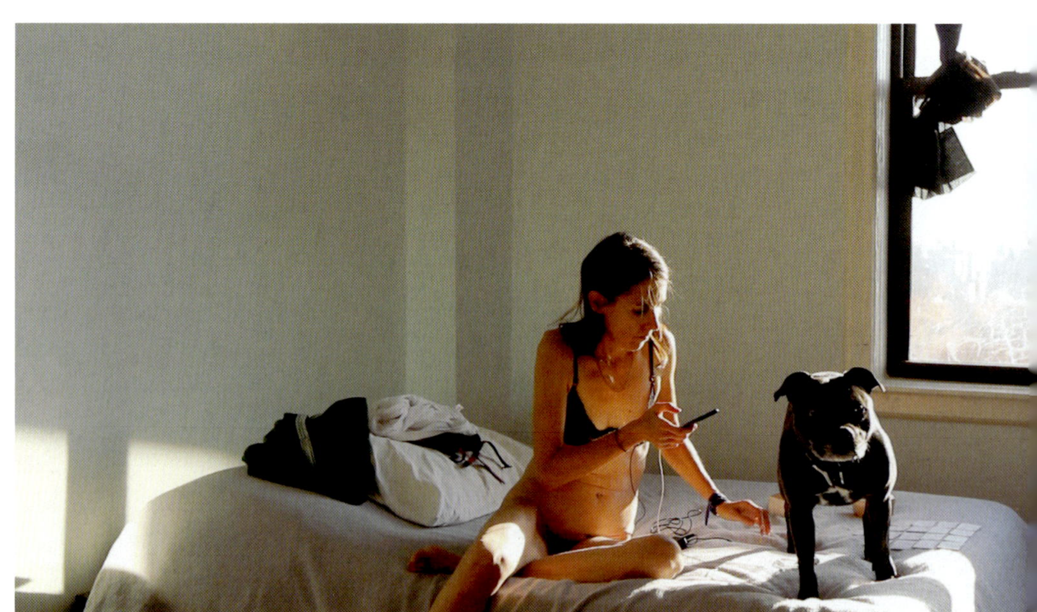

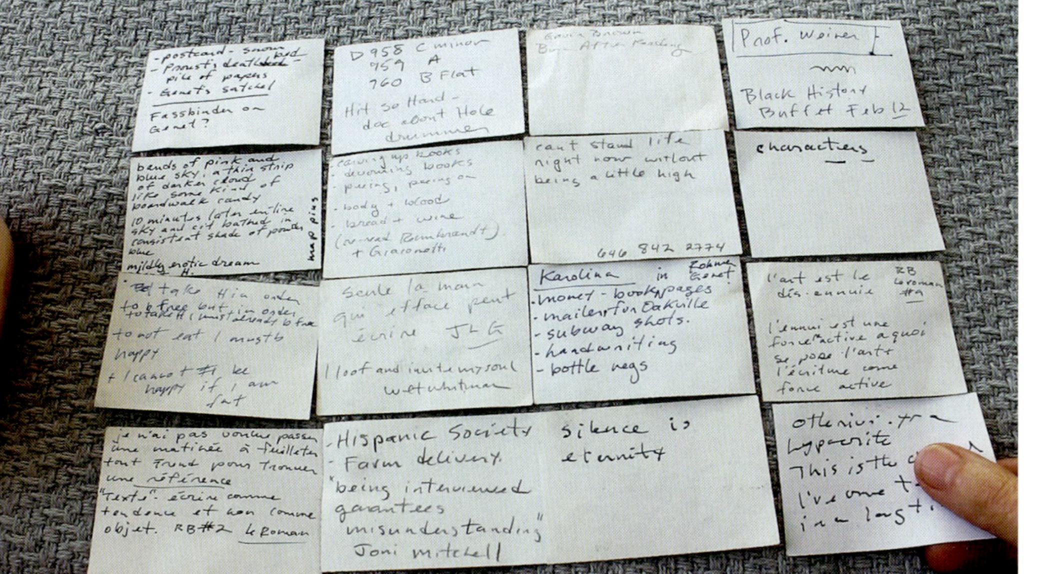
- postcard - snow
- pile of papers
- Genet's satchel
Fassbinder on Genet?
D958 C minor
959 A
760 B Flat
Hit so Hard - doc about Hole drummer
Prof. Weiner
Black History Buffet Feb 12
bands of pink and blue sky, a thin strip of darker cloud
like some kind of boardwalk candy
mildly erotic dream
map pins
· body + blood
· bread + wine
+ Giacometti
cant stand life right now without being a little high
646 842 2774
characters
to not eat I must be happy
+ I cannot be happy if I am fat
Seule la main qui efface peut écrire JLG
I loaf and invite my soul walt whitman
Karolina
· money - book pages
· mailer for Oakville
· subway shots.
· handwriting
· bottle negs
l'art est le dés-ennui
RB le roman #9
l'ennui est une force active à quoi se pose l'art + l'écriture comme force active
je n'ai pas voulu passer une matinée à feuilleter tout Freud pour trouver une référence
"Texte": écrire comme tendance et non comme objet. RB #2 le Roman
- Hispanic Society
- Farm delivery.
"being interviewed garantees misunderstanding"
Joni Mitchell
silence is eternity
hypocrite
This is the

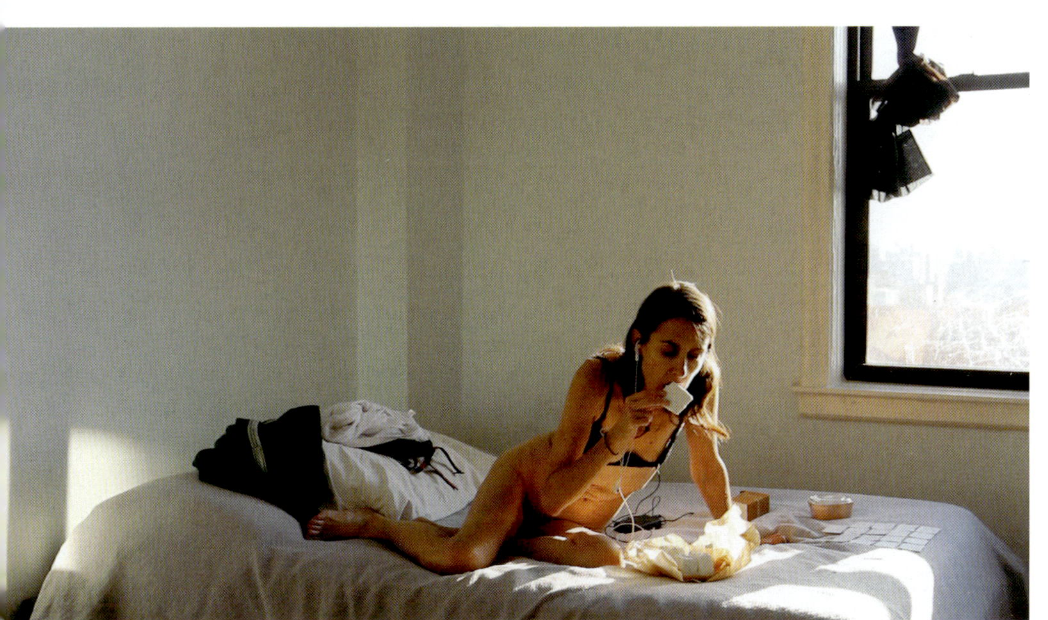

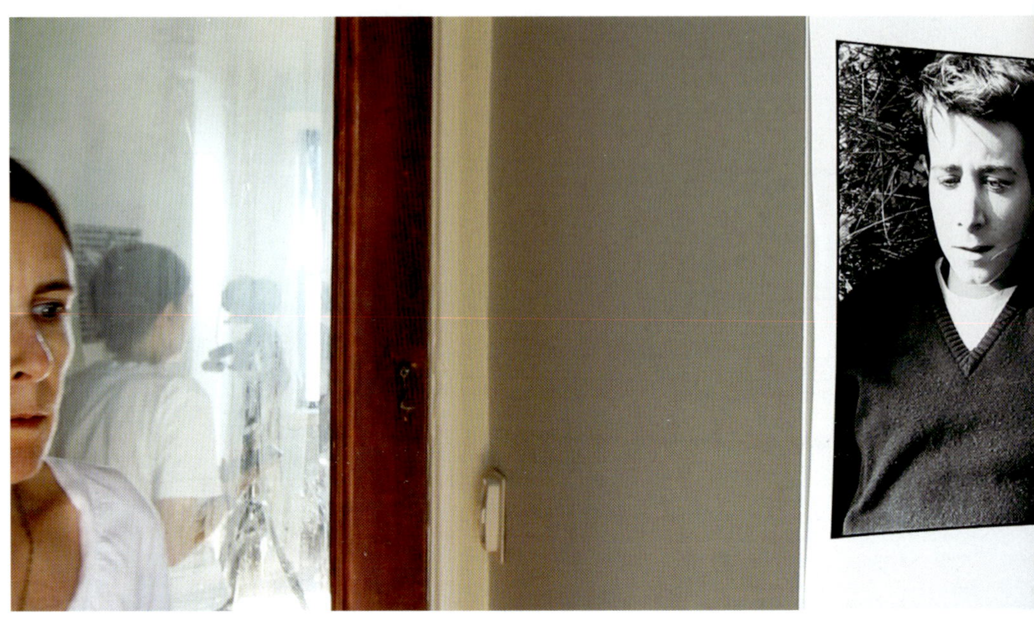

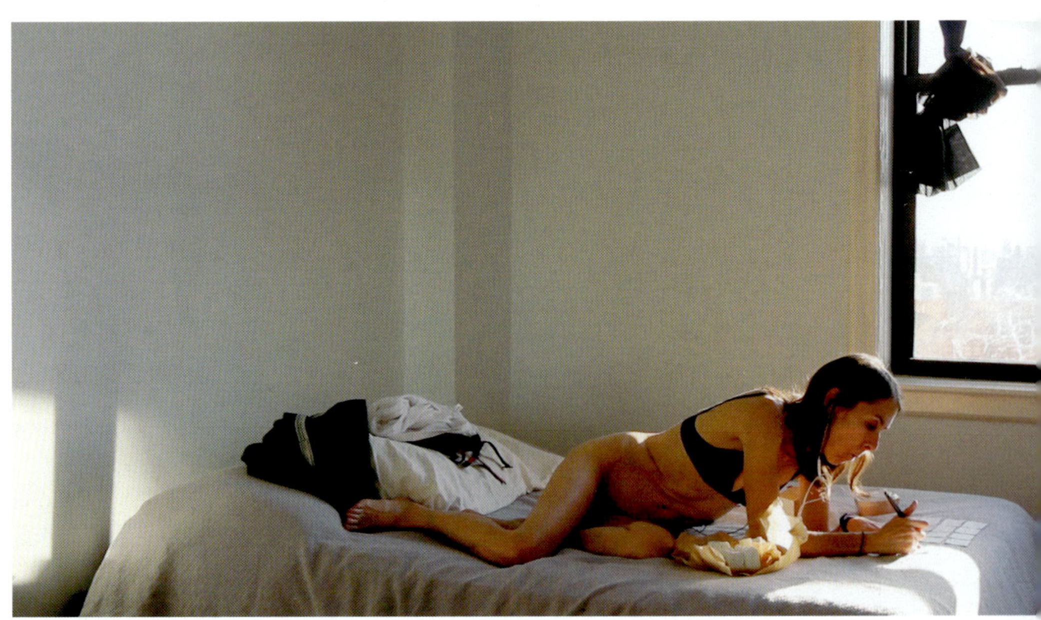

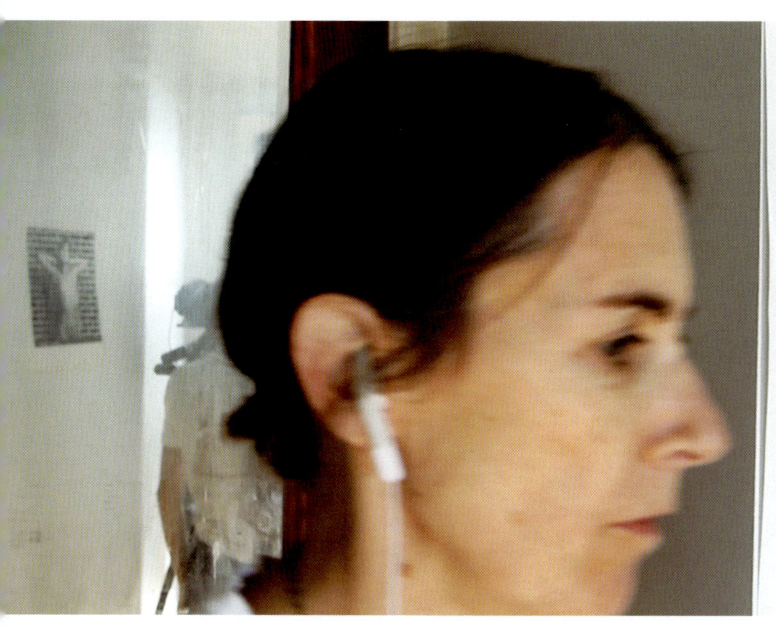
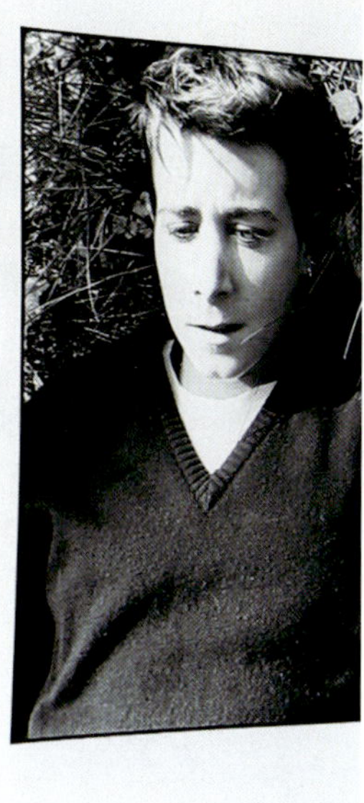
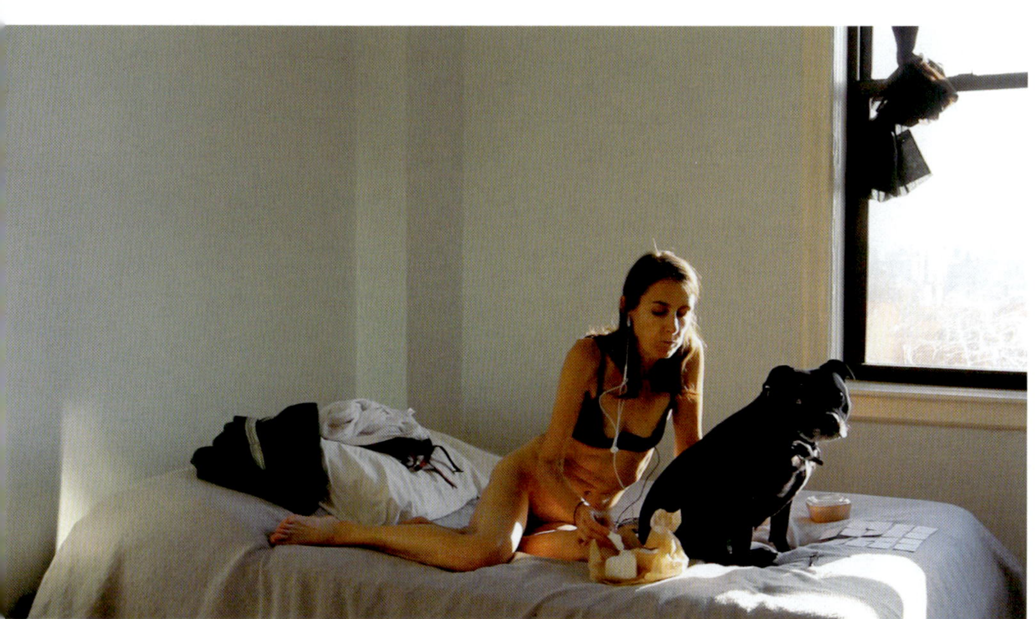

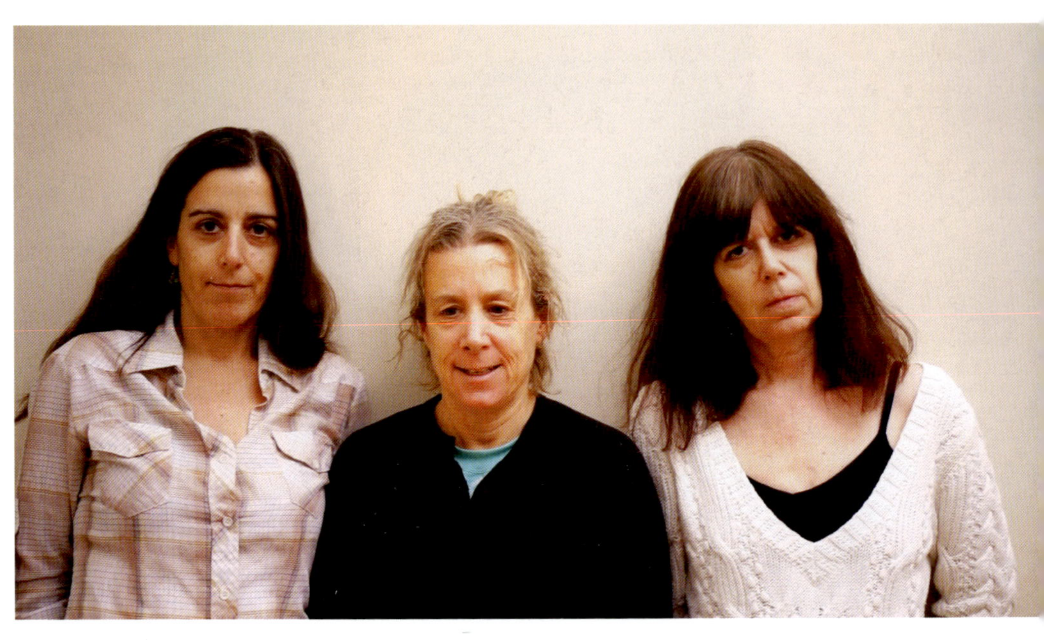

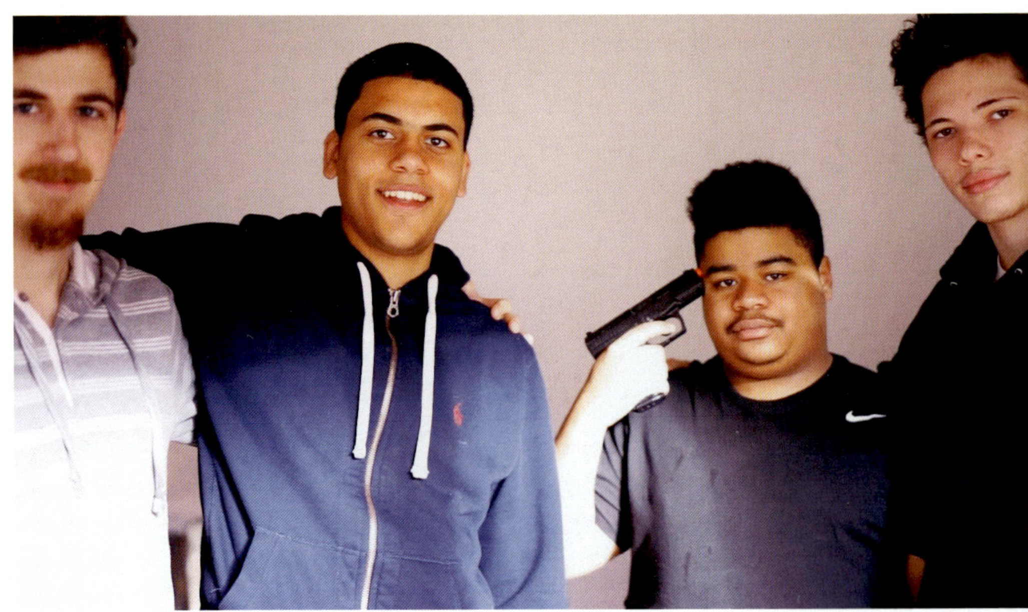

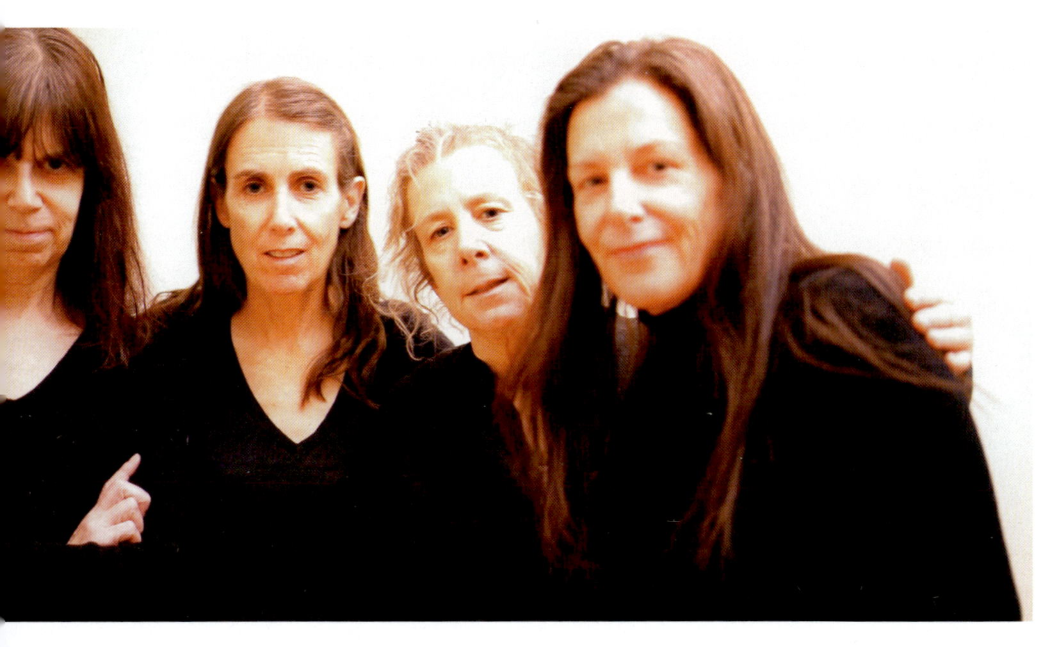

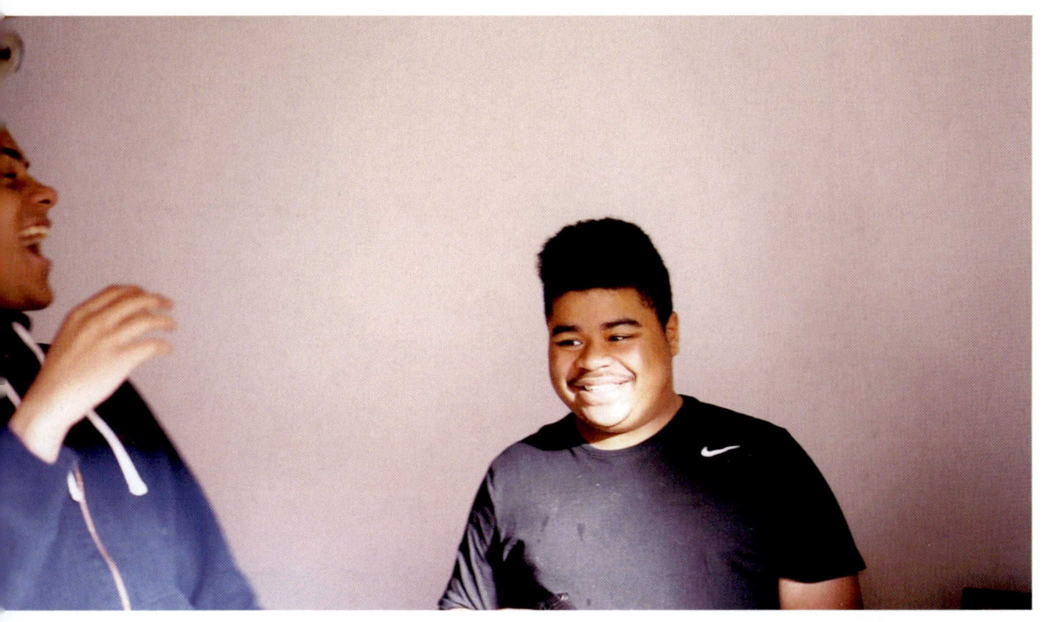

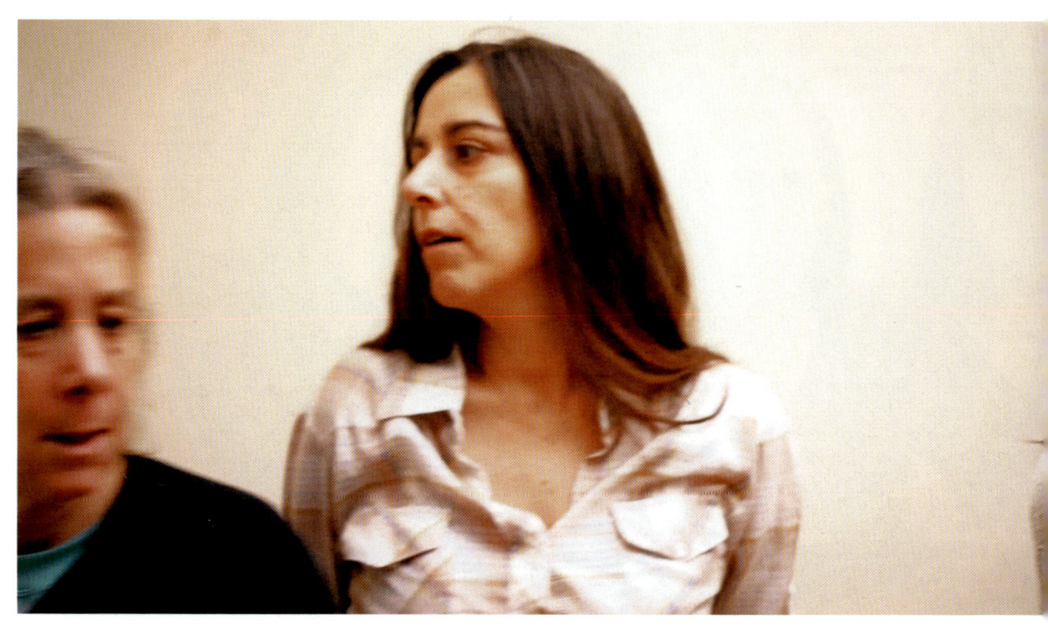

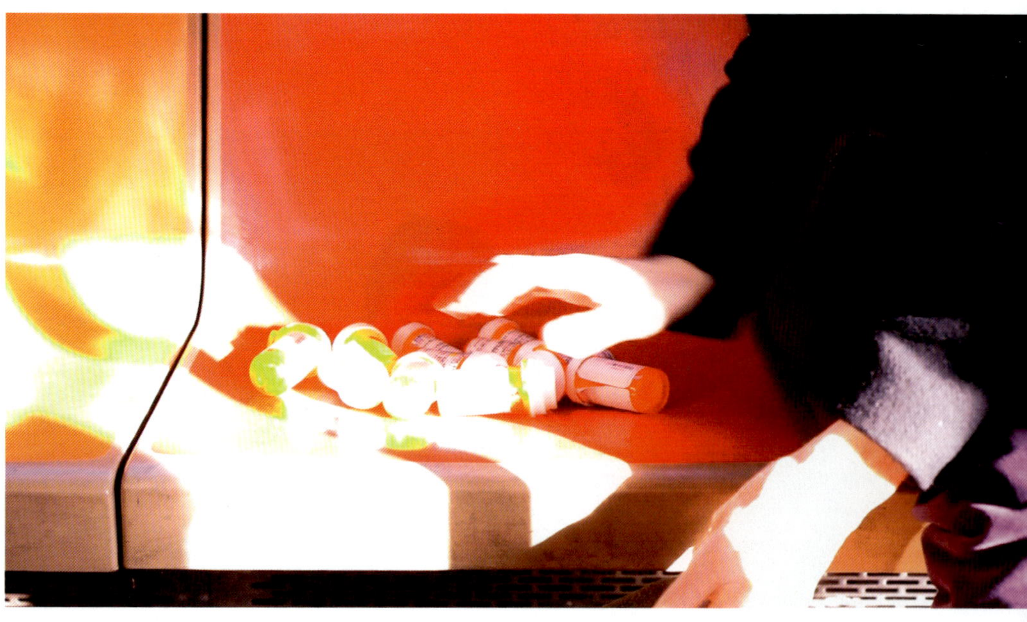

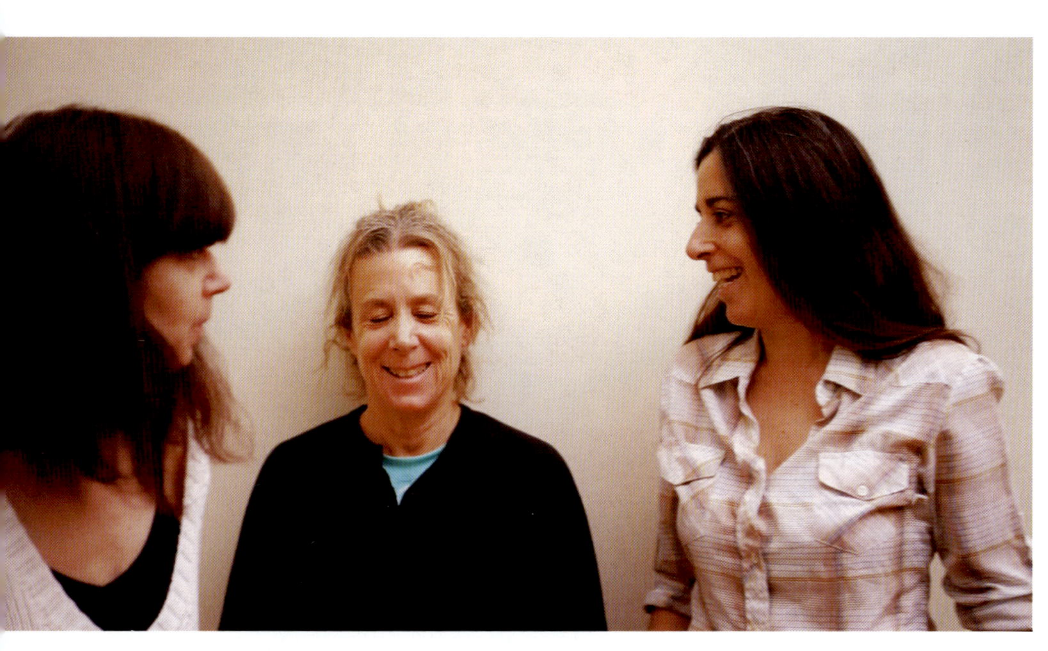

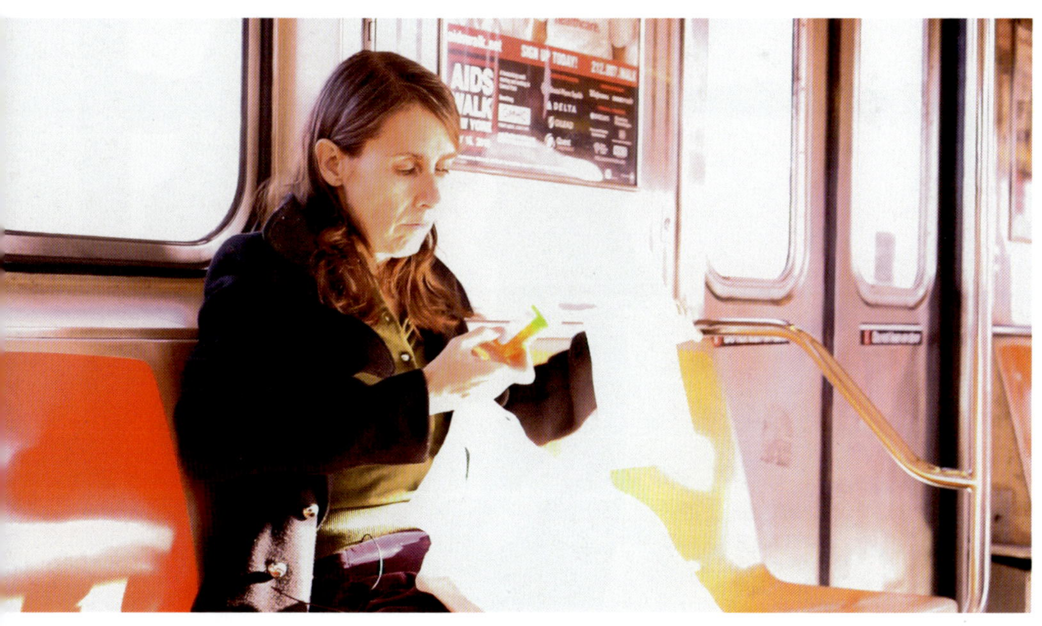
SIGN UP TODAY!
AIDS
WALK
DELTA

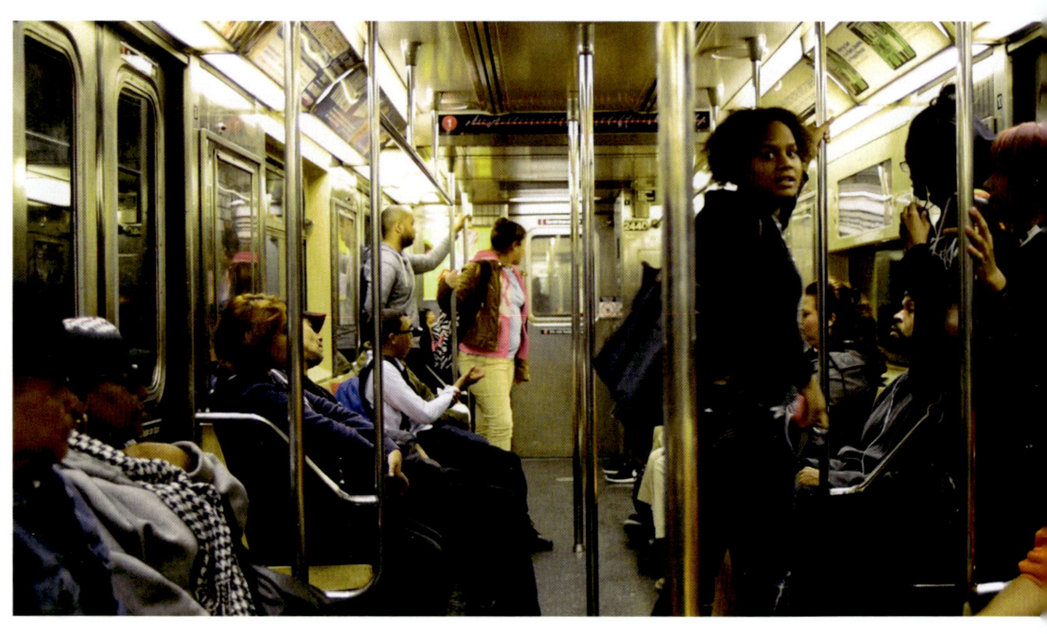

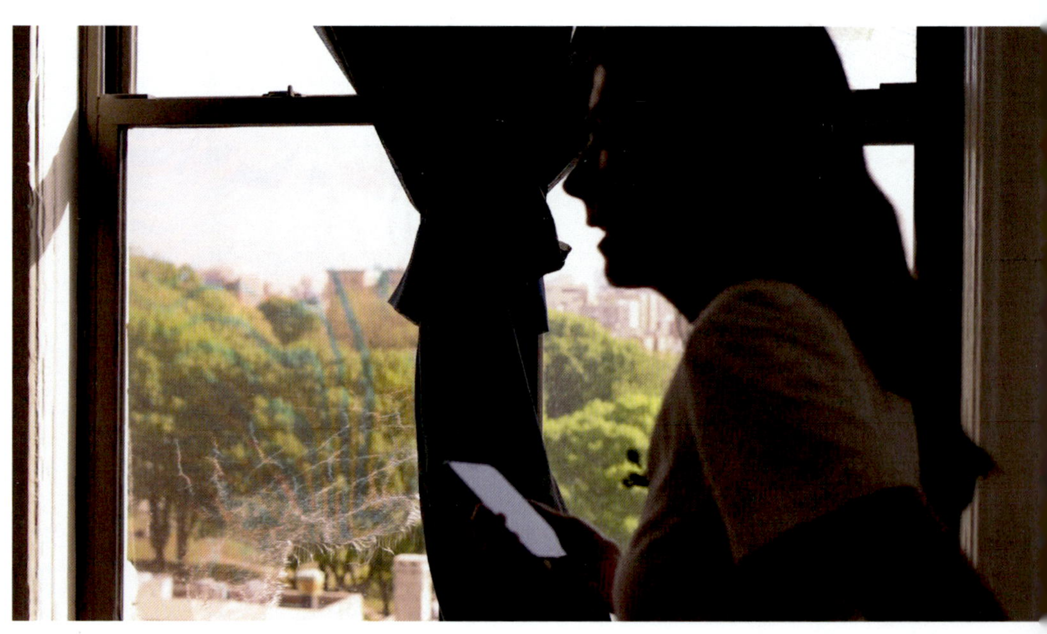

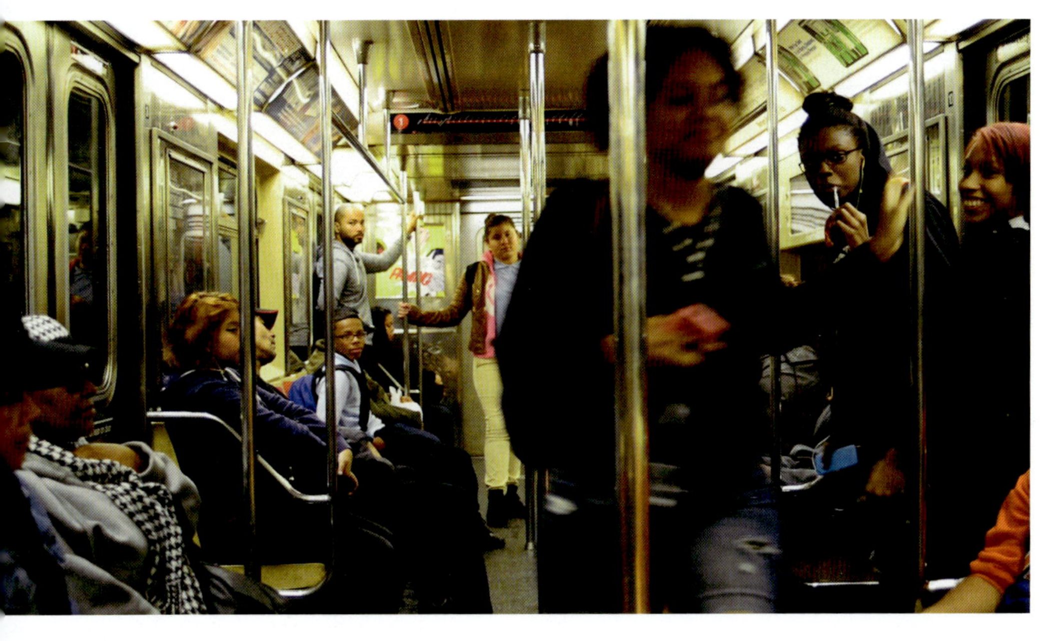

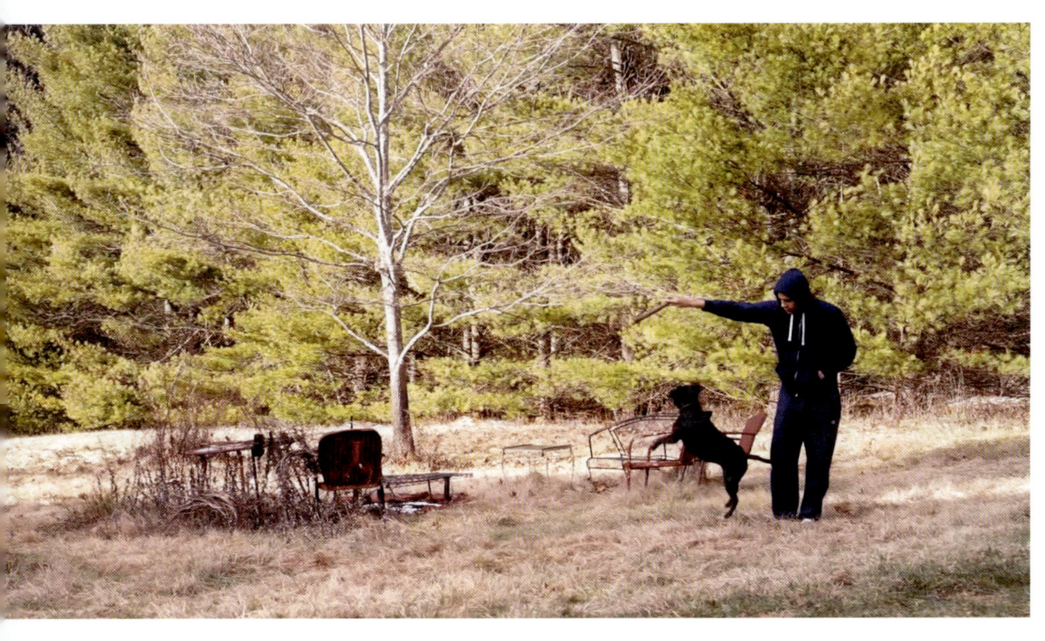

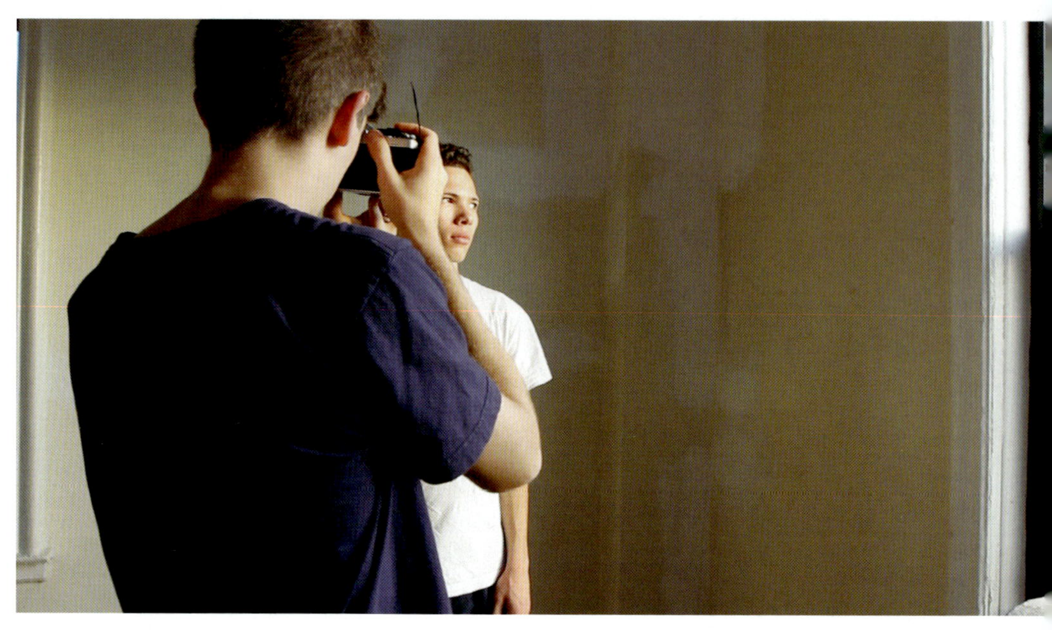

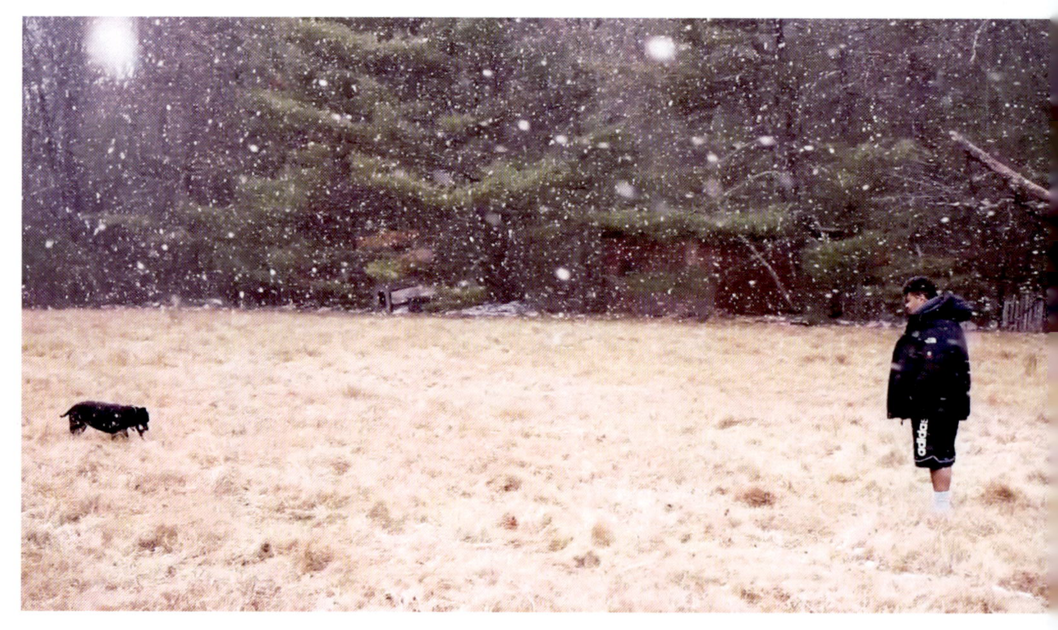
adidas

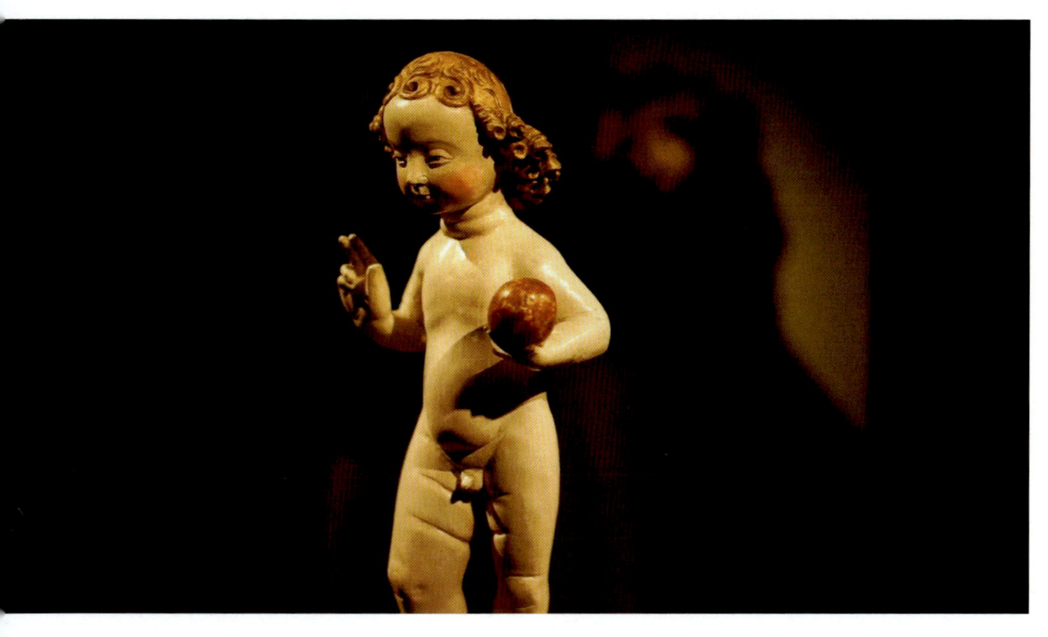

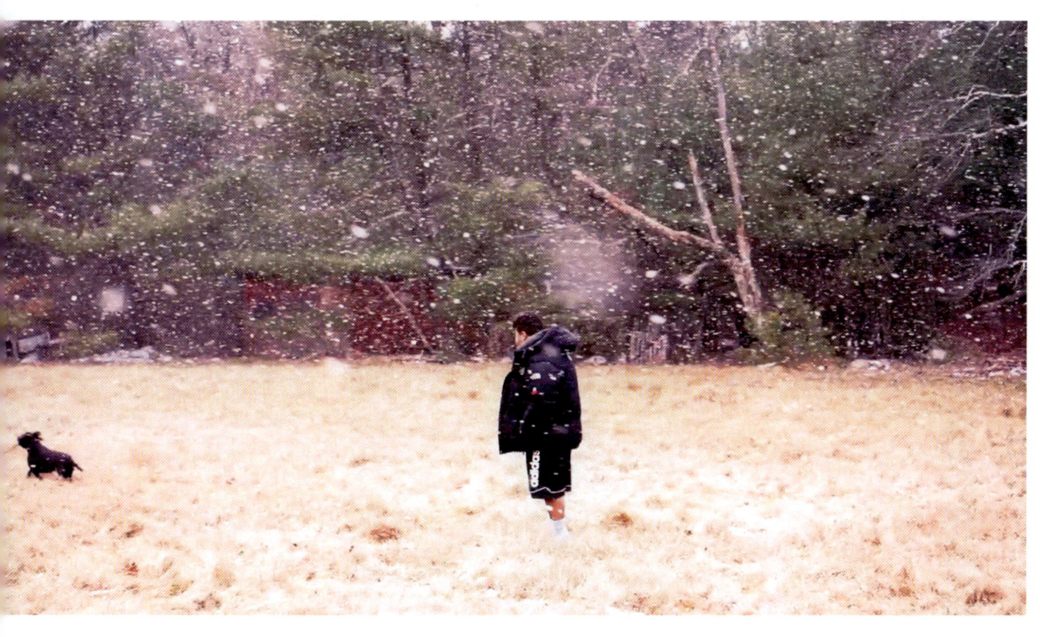

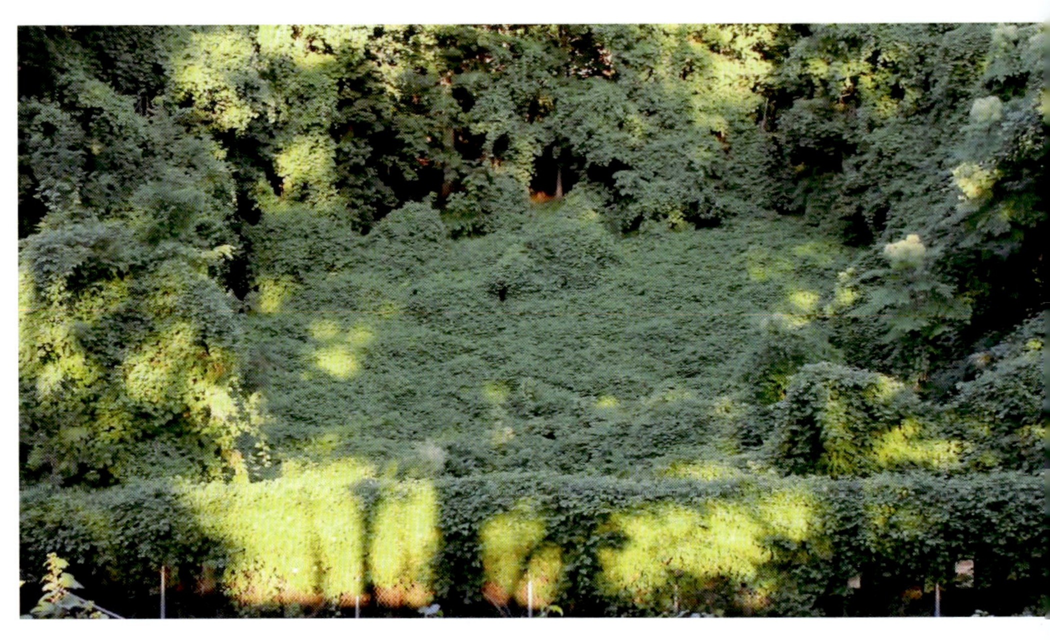

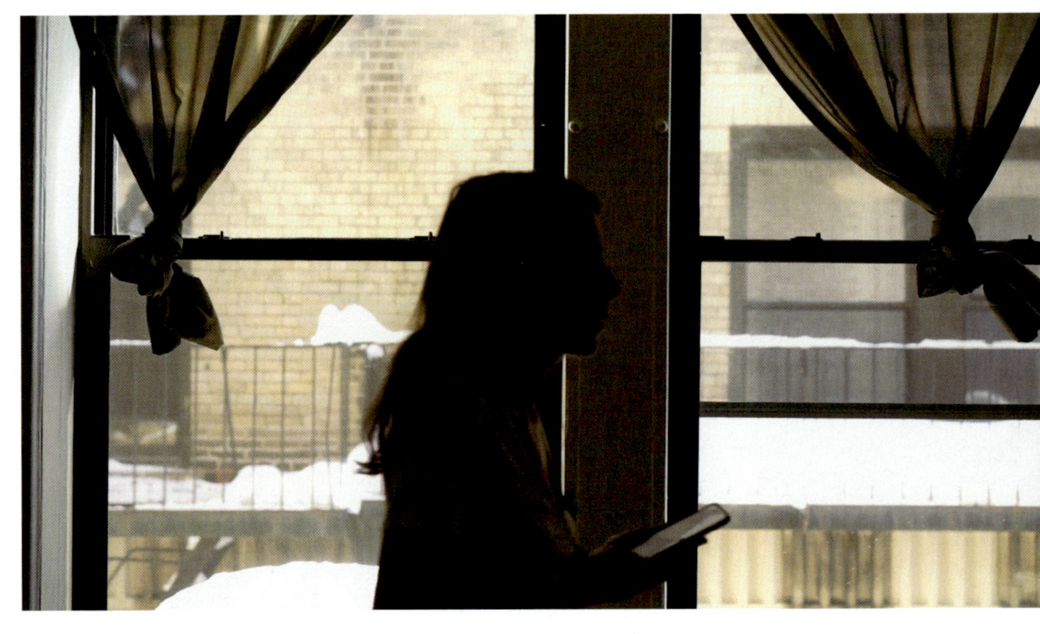

MOYRA DAVEY

Hemlock Forest

NEWS

News from Home by Chantal Akerman comprises breathtaking views of Manhattan accompanied by the filmmaker's voice reading her mother's letters from Brussels. These are frequently melancholic, pleading, a mother desperate for news of an apparently unresponsive daughter living on her own in what was then a dangerous city. Shot on film, *News* is saturated with gorgeous color, and Babette Mangolte's camera work is a thing of beauty.

A third of the way into the film, there's a subway shot aimed straight down the 1 train. The camera is uncannily still, taking in the movements of passengers, some curious, most indifferent, and one man dressed in lime green, apparently annoyed. Taken aback, he lurches, scowls at the camera, then turns on his heel and walks quickly away through the open doors into the next car.

I have an urge to re-create the scene by asking cinematographers to film a contemporary version of the shot. But I immediately begin to feel anxious and depressed about the idea: this is not how I've worked, I've always done my own scenes, even if this type of unpredictable situation in public is where I am most challenged technically. The idea of filming this quasi-illegal scene both makes me sick with nerves and—if I can pull it off—is a huge rush. This scene is the opposite of "low-hanging fruit."

I do in fact go out and shoot the scene, first with Jason and then with a camerawoman, Liz Sales. I am on edge for a week before the shoot with Liz, even having dreams about it. But we do it. We get the shot, with the doors open between two cars on the 1 train. We do it without permission, and no one says a word except three rowdy girls who gently heckle from behind the camera.

KUDZU

In *Goodbye to Language*, we hear a male voice ask off camera: "To live one's life or to tell it?" Not long ago, I asked my son if he kept a diary, and he answered: "I'd rather live my life than narrate it."

I'm piecing together fragments because I don't yet have a subject.

A French writer said apropos of fragments, "choosing is easier than inventing," and wondered how he might pass from notes and fragments to the novel. He speculated that he was breaking the ultimate rule of writers—speaking about a nascent work—and that his "work" might in the end be the notes on its making. In that same lecture, he mentioned how much he delighted in hearing *any* professional talk about their craft, in detail, and how rare this was.

I might in fact have a subject, but it feels raw and intractable. A part of me is leaving at the very moment he is becoming a person. He rides me on his bicycle so that I can film the kudzu jungle in Riverside Park. I cling to his shoulder with one hand and hold the camera aloft with the other.

DEATH

The morning after the subway shot, I learn of Akerman's death. A friend tells me she was mourning the loss of her mother, who is also the subject of her last film. Apparently her mother's death was supposed to free Chantal, but it had the opposite effect. I remember Annette Michelson years ago publicly interviewing Akerman, who quietly wept over the misfortune of having made a perfect film at age twenty-five. That film is the epic *Jeanne Dielman*, about a housewife who lives alone with her son, imprisoned by her home and the routine of its maintenance.

I perform some lines from *A Doll's House*, another story about a woman, Nora, trapped in her home, subjugated to a condescending husband who treats her like a child, who talks to her as though she were his little pet: "Is that skylark chirping out there? Has little bird been frittering money again?" I narrate these and similar lines from the play four or five times before I realize they aren't working. The light is fading, but I persist, wearing myself out. And I squander the blue robin's egg in the process.

In the frame, just above the TV, there's a small paperback copy of Tillie Olsen's *Silences.* I keep staring at it and eventually start to think of Käthe Kollwitz, whom Olsen includes in the collection, writing about working in her studio after her children have left home. I read the passage to J. over the phone: "I am gradually approaching the period in my life when work comes first. . . . No longer diverted by other emotions, I work the way a cow grazes . . . and yet formerly, in my so wretchedly limited working time, I was more productive, because I was more sensual." I start to cry at the word *sensual.*

This passage, included in a book I edited eighteen years ago called *Mother Reader*, has stayed with me, a harbinger. And now Kollwitz's reality is upon me, as is the reality of Akerman's mother when Chantal moved to New York and didn't answer her letters.

SOUND

Even more captivating than my laments from the journals are other writers' words, loosely transcribed, such as these from a Norwegian novelist. He said: "Sound is the present, ever-changing; silence is eternity." He said that in relation to the remote shores of Newfoundland, and the contrasting stillness as he retreated from the surf.

As a child, he is surrounded by forest, with its smells and rot, its filtered light and colors. The protective canopy of the woods is his giant playground and refuge.

Another of my notes cites an American composer and pianist discussing in the *Brooklyn Rail* "the difference between seeing a tree and seeing/recording a tree through a view finder."

I set a camera on the dash, pointing at the trees and vines along the Palisades. As I steal glances at the tiny screen, the shots seem promising, but when I look at them later they are absolutely ordinary. I call this type of filming "low-hanging fruit," and it rarely adds up to much because so little is at stake.

ADDICTED

Addicted to work to forget that:
I can't sleep.
I can't shit.
My stomach hurts.
My hands burn.
I piss in the saddle.
I miss my son.

In the days and weeks after your death, we all stream and watch your films and interviews. Elisabeth posts on her blog *Le beau vice* a heartbreaking tribute and describes loving the sound of your voice. You talked about using your body in your films, and how you could never get actors to adequately substitute for your clumsiness. I watch *Je tu il elle*, in which you shovel powdered sugar into your mouth while writing lying down. Eventually you disrobe and pad about the nearly empty room, naked. You look directly into the camera and smile.

You became a filmmaker because of Godard, but later turned against him, called him an anti-Semite.

I spend hours watching you online, listening to you talk about Proust, about Judaism, and, always, about your mother, who "came out of the camps," as you put it. In Jerusalem, you school out film students, call them "spoiled children." You tell the young women not to be afraid of making things that aren't beautiful. I too cannot get enough of your raspy smoker's voice. You're fearless and charismatic, and I could listen to you

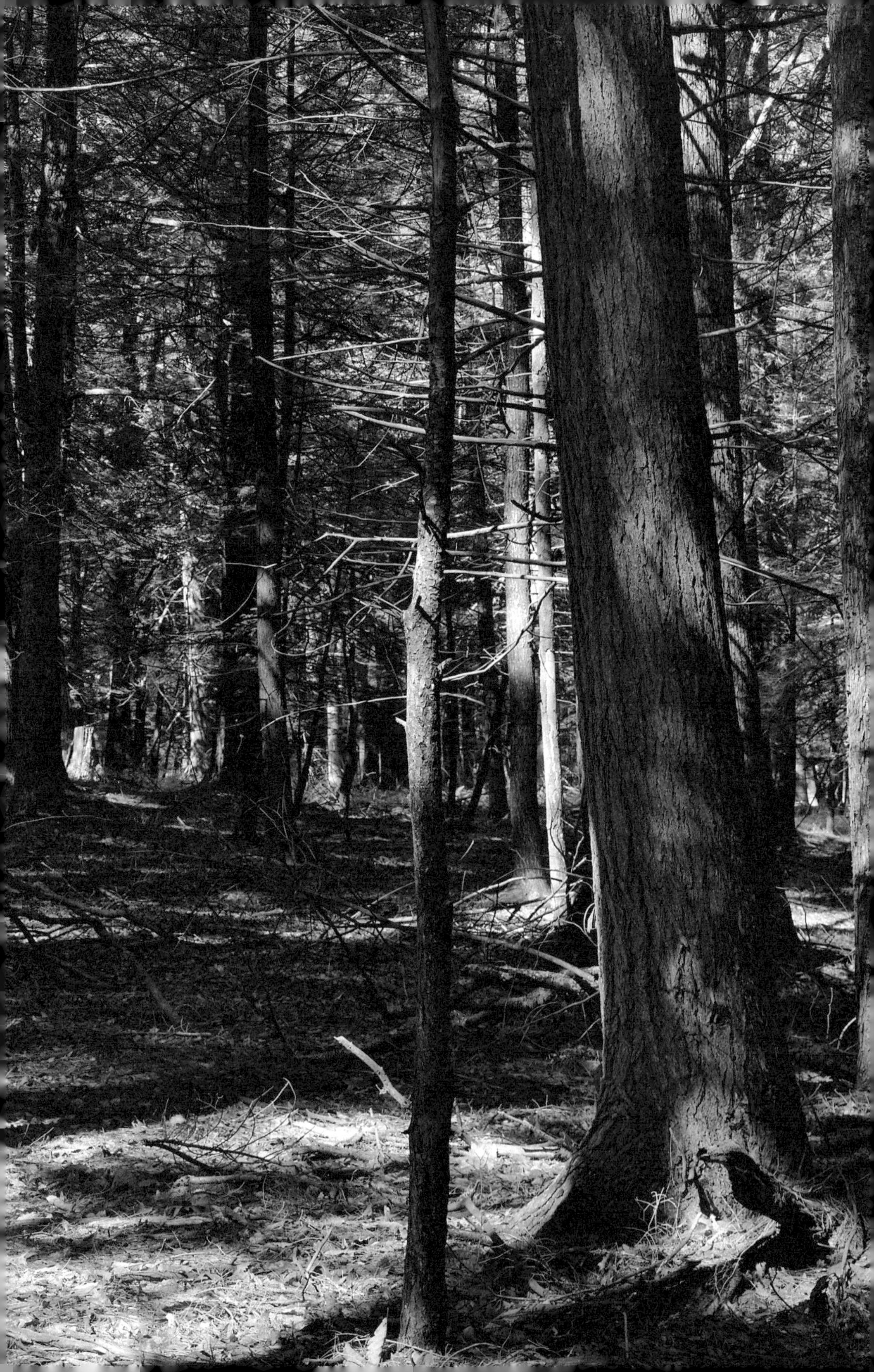

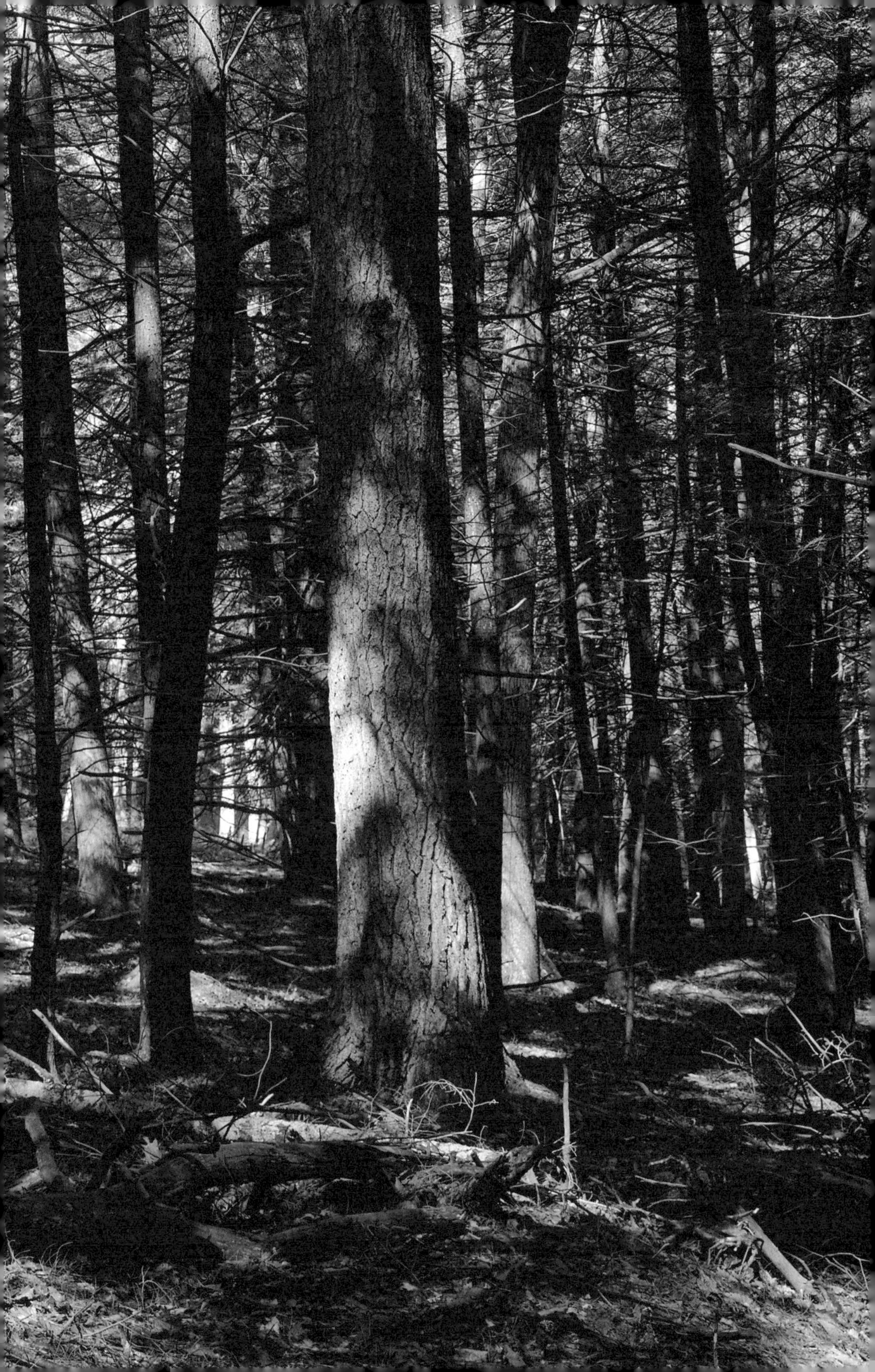

forever. I search for more. Eventually it sinks in that you're no longer here to give us more.

MARY

When Mary Wollstonecraft visited Sweden and Norway in 1795, she drank the landscape. Its beauty was a tonic to her depression and sadness, and she bore witness in her letters to the restorative effects of the rugged coastline, the giant trees, and the marvels of sunlight.

The love of her life, her soul mate, and the father of her small child had moved on. He was doing his best to get rid of her, and her desperation over unanswered letters sent from abroad is conveyed in no uncertain terms. At the conclusion of the voyage by land and sea, after experiencing "the effusions of a sensibility wounded almost to madness," Mary tried to end her life. She was rescued from drowning, and then, while convalescing, proceeded to craft the letters into what would become her best-selling work, *Letters Written during a Short Residence in Sweden, Norway, and Denmark.* At this point, she was also in a new relationship with William Godwin, who offered this advice to Mary: "A disappointed woman should try to construct happiness 'out of a set of materials within [her] reach.'"

DERAILED

I am now officially derailed by Chantal Akerman. I read Ivone Margulies, who loves Chantal and has written a thoughtful, analytic book on her, in the course of which it is necessary to mention terms and phrases familiar to me from the eighties and nineties, such as:

Cinematic praxis
Freud's Dora
Lacanian theory
Reified allegory
Reflexivity
Split nature of subjectivity
Strategies of distanciation
Subject formation
To-be-looked-at-ness
Visibility
Visuality
Will to allegory

I still don't know what some of these word combinations mean, and I feel the hairs go up on my back as I remember the policing and posturing that went on then, and certain boring films that got made by way of enacting these theories.

You shied away from most labels except "feminist," at least when it came to *Jeanne Dielman*. You spoke about your films enigmatically, in an idiom that was completely your own. You said, in 1982, "I haven't tried to find a compromise between myself and others. I have thought that the more particular I am, the more I address the general."

JANE

William Godwin's phrase about a disappointed woman has engraved itself on my psyche, and inevitably when I think of it, it is my sister Jane, one year older than me, who bore three children and lost one to an accidental overdose a few months before her twentieth birthday, who comes to mind. Days after

Hannah died, Jane left her relationship of thirteen years and moved to my mother's house, where she continues to write her memoir of addiction.

The manuscript has undergone countless revisions, but Jane has decided against writing about Hannah. She is taking care of my mother and taking care of herself, and whether or not happiness is a realistic goal, as Freud put it, she is trying to construct peace "out of a set of materials within her reach."

Yet here *I* am talking about Hannah, born in 1993, two hundred years (minus one) after Mary Wollstonecraft's first daughter, Fanny, who also died of an overdose of opiates, at age twenty-two, though in her case it was deliberate.

SHAME

I have been immersed in K. like a drug. The foreignness has something to do with it: I can more readily give myself over to contemporary fiction where the translator has left in traces of a Scandinavian accent.

K. goes in and out of aggression and soporific benevolence. At times, he is a cranky misanthrope, boldly calling out individuals who've crossed him. Then suddenly it's as though a bad mood lifts, and he is a different person: kind, even-keeled, pacific. He writes with tenderness about caring for his small children.

I have been trying to locate his shame in all of this, but so far I see it only in drunkenness. Add to this the fact that when transgressions figure in literature they've already been transformed.

In real life, I've judged my friends for their drinking and my sister for being a party girl; to my shame, I even inwardly faulted her for falling off the wagon in the wake of Hannah. Jane wrote to me: "I can't stand life right now without being a little high."

This brings me to something important, of which I must constantly remind my judgmental self: take the good with the bad; otherwise you're a hypocrite.

FILMING

In her letters, steeped in Kantian images of the sublime, Mary Wollstonecraft exults in the beauty and restorative powers of the natural world. She was briefly rescued, kept alive, by the lush forests of Scandinavia.

Mary's published book *Letters* is also firmly rooted in the social. Its author is a reporter, receiving a culture and its people with all her sensibilities heightened. Mary's radical principles and her recent memories of revolutionary France inflect all her writings.

I'm reliant on the words of others, and I glom on to the dead. In the car, driving north on the Palisades, I listen to music, much of it Barney's, but then Bryan Ferry comes on singing Dylan, and it reminds me that we all sample, we all do covers, and that it's a way of expressing love and allegiance. Taking in but also giving back.

A woman rabbi gives the eulogy for Chantal. She recounts an anecdote of you filming your last birthday party in the hospital before finally putting down the camera and saying: "Non, maintenant il me faut vivre et pas juste filmer." ("No, now I must live life and not just film it.")

The trouble is you can only "live" once you've filmed. That feeling of freedom and release comes only after you've worked very hard for it. Years after making *Hotel Monterey*, you remembered the feeling: "I can breathe, I'm really a filmmaker."

IMAN ISSA

A few years ago, Iman Issa wrote, "Watching Moyra Davey's film [*Les Goddesses*] I had the feeling that I was confronted with more than just the work of an artist, a photographer, or a woman reflecting on her life and profession. Her often repeated 'I' didn't come across as the 'I' of a therapeutic self-portrait, or the timid and humble 'I' of a self-reflexive gesture. Davey's 'I' felt more desperate, more like a last resort. Perhaps she has known for quite some time that this voice is one of the few, if not the only, with which it is still possible to speak."

When I read Issa's description, in particular her use of the word *desperate*, I feel she'd put her finger on it, and I am impressed by her forthrightness in calling me out. I am still trying to parse the "desperate 'I' of last resort" and why it felt to her like the only viable one. Perhaps it's because it signals a risk being taken.

I was in fact frantic when I wrote parts of *Les Goddesses.* My body was breaking down. I peed in front of the ATM; the raking light in the morning, the cold, the pervasive frostiness of French teachers, and the humiliation of mediocre report cards were being visited on Barney.

Desperate has evolved. Now there is the vanity of self-preservation, in the sense that if I push myself too hard I become depleted, gaunt. "What's the *use* of working oneself to death . . . " But like most in my situation I need to keep working to live, and not just materially, because, as Ibsen said, "I've come to realize [I'll never] find happiness in idle pleasure."

LOVE LETTER

Les Goddesses was a love letter to my family. I linked my sisters to Mary and her siblings, my parents to hers. I forged a coincidence of dates two hundred years apart to make connections and enable a story. I've often wondered what it would mean to revisit that account, word for word, showing us as we are now, not via pictures taken thirty-five years ago when the Davey girls were in their heyday and when my mother went on record saying, "I'd mind less [about the sex] if I thought they enjoyed it more." A lot has changed since then. Things didn't exactly work out for some of us. Intoxication lasted longer and played harder for some of us. We didn't come through those party days unscathed.

Excepting the occasional rueful aside, my mother made a point not to speak about her children, and like her I've been circumspect. But now the boy is suddenly a man with one foot out the door and plays his cards close to his chest. He relaxed and opened up once over a bottle of champagne; he sat and talked for an hour, and I could see the tension drain from his face. Then something a bit more innocent happened: he put his head in my lap like a living Pietà. He was slightly high. I'd been dying to hold him in my arms and squeeze his flesh like the chubby baby he'd once been. I said, "You're a nice guy to let me hold you like this."

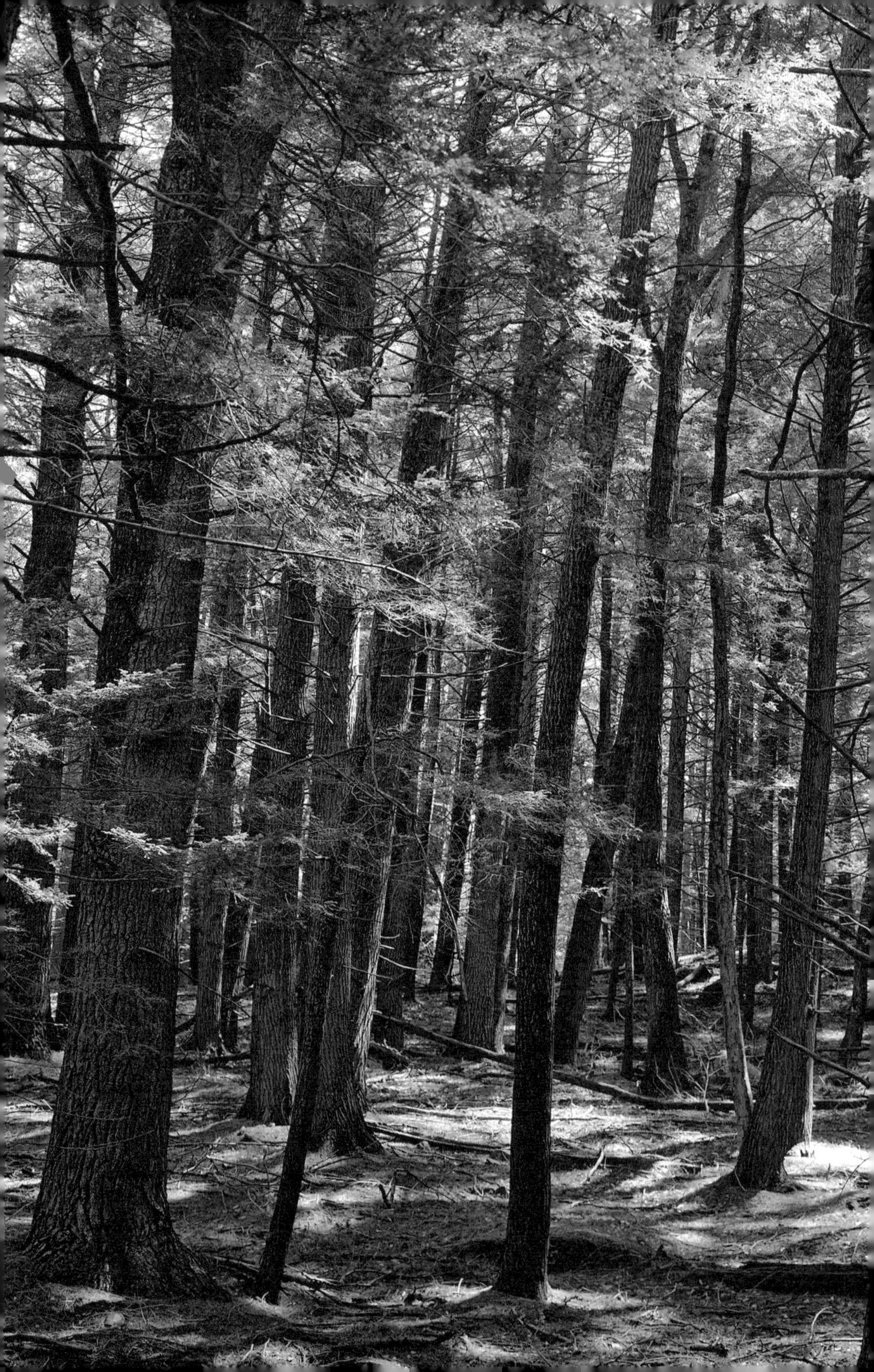

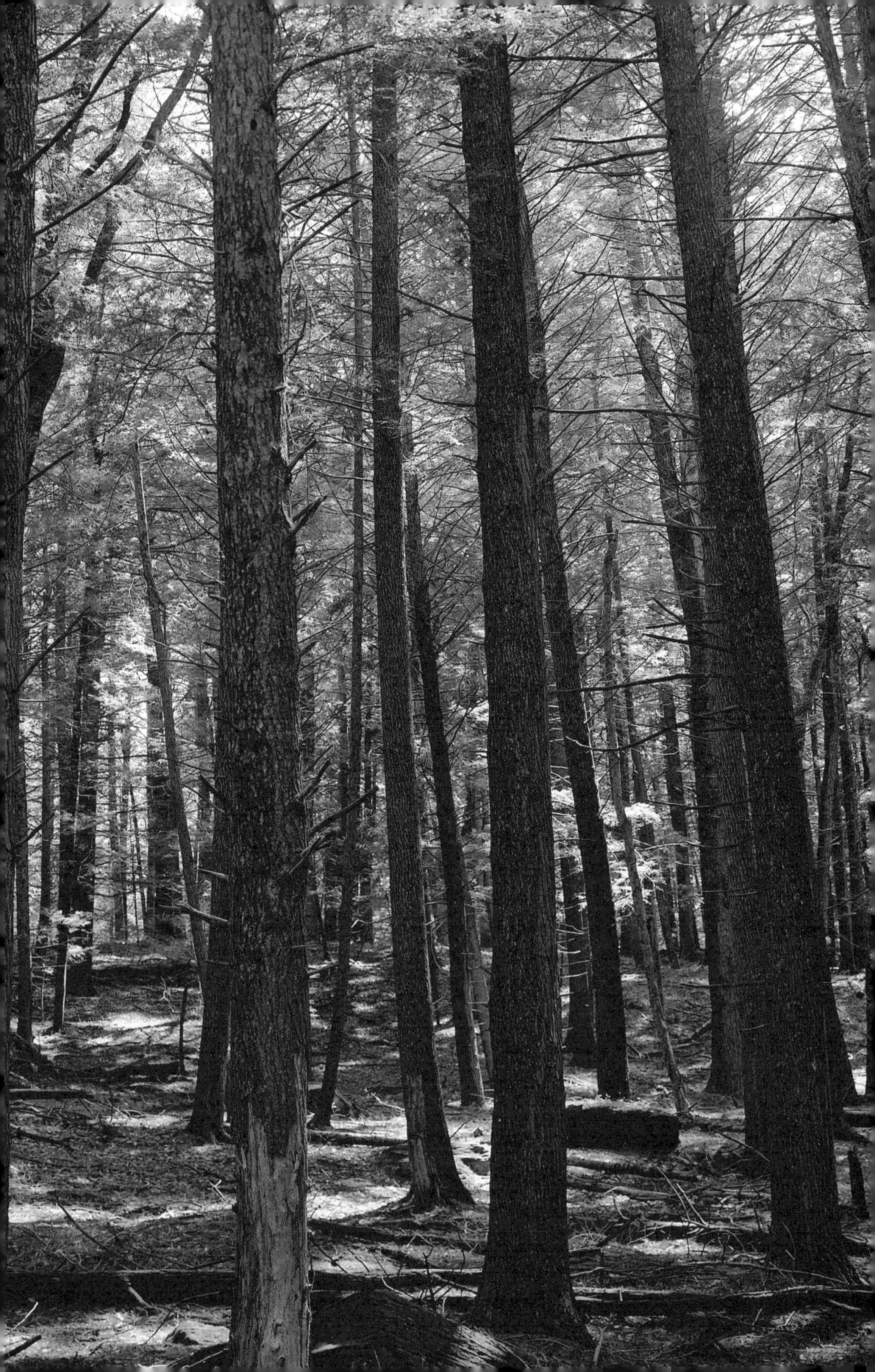

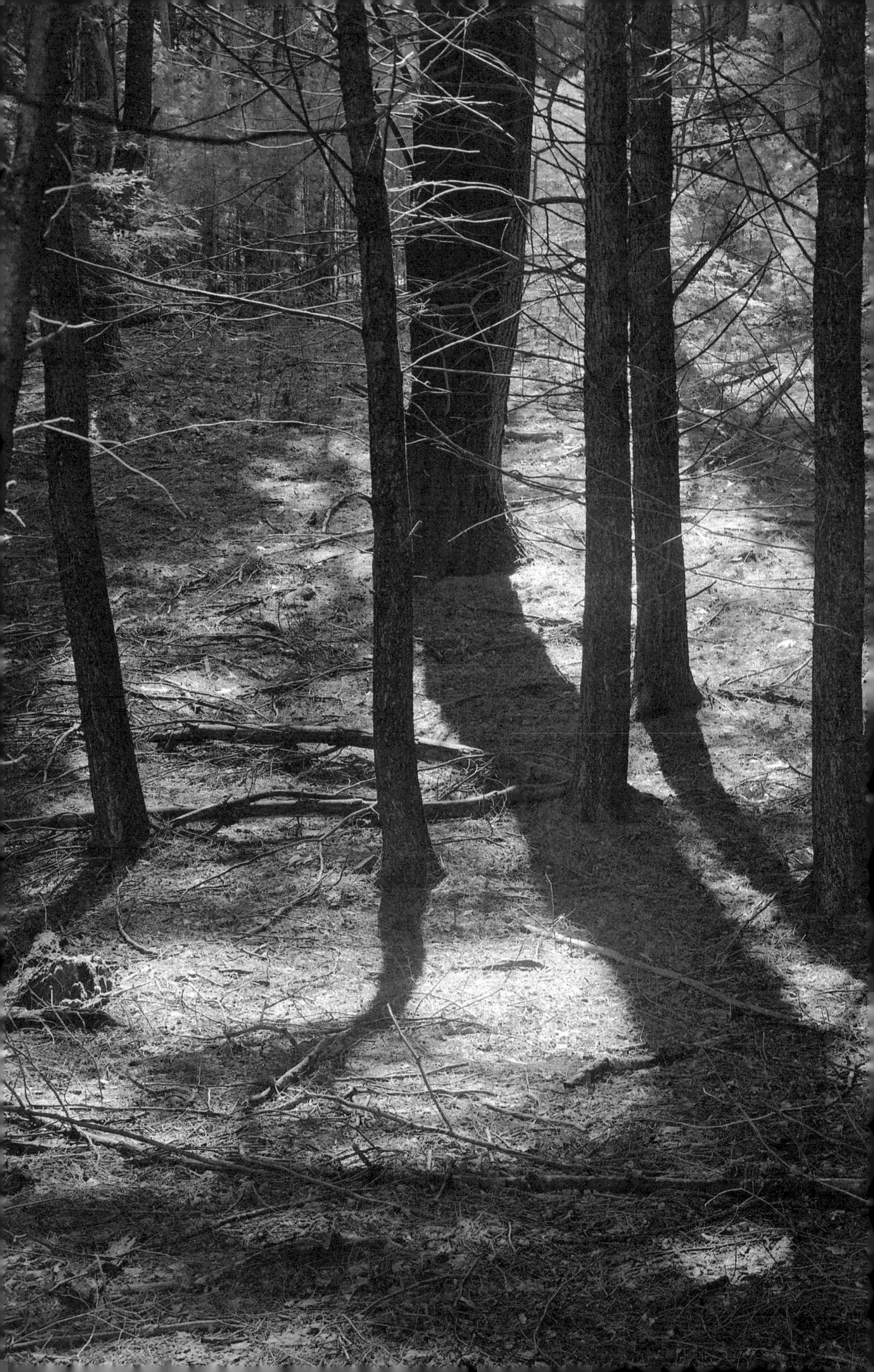

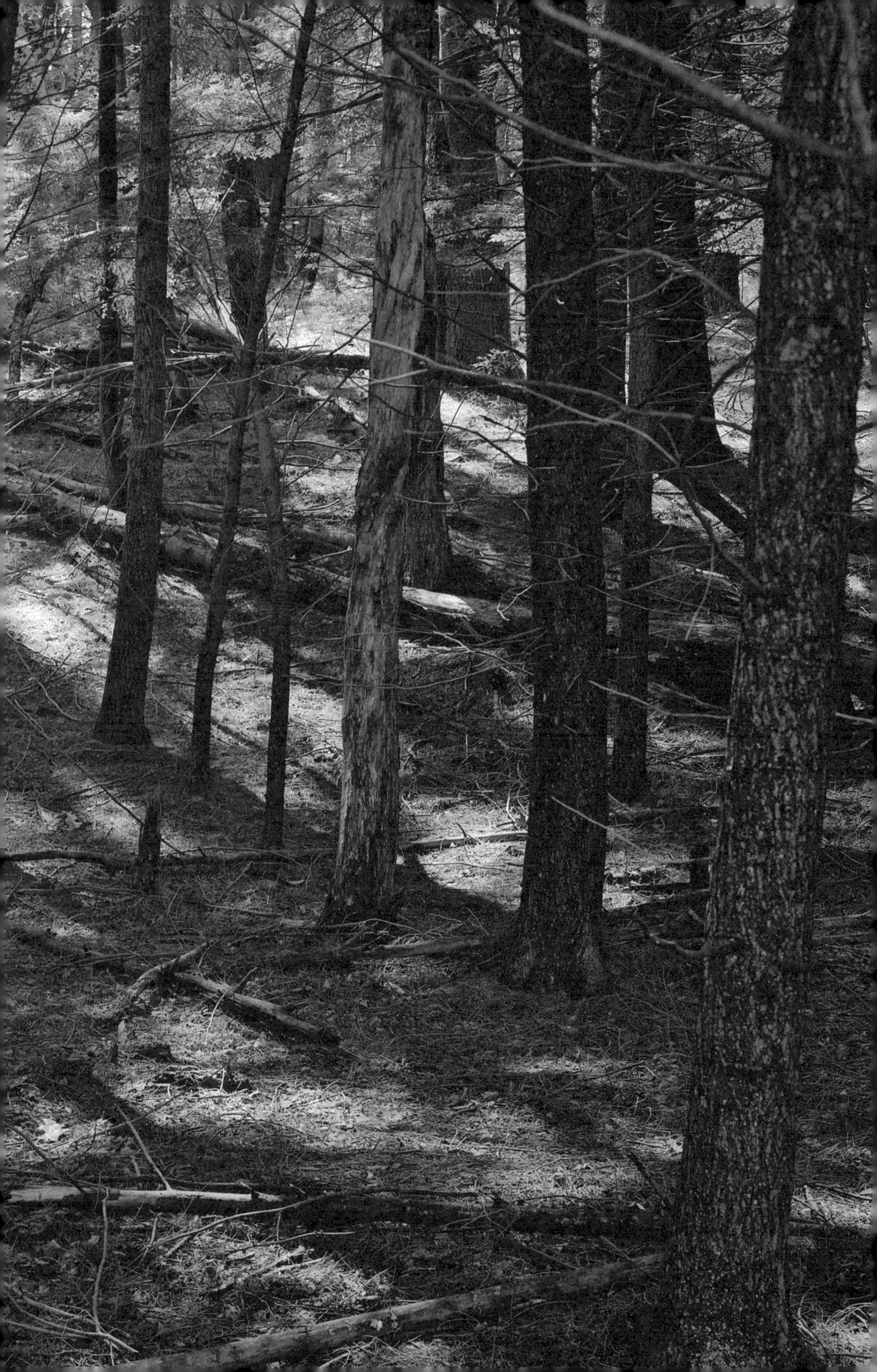

ELISABETH

Elisabeth asked, apropos of my book from 2001, "If you were doing *Mother Reader* now, what would you include?" Inevitably I've also been queried about "empty nest," a tough one to consider because the advent of it is so clichéd, the emotions strong and real.

I hear, echoing in the public hallway, the wail of a child pleading for its mother. This type of anguish goes straight to my nerve center, spiriting me back to childhood, my own and Barney's. I remember my transgressions, the times when Barney was that unhappy child. But I'm also pretty sure, as per Winnicott, that I was "good enough."

You are riding your bike in the park at dusk, struck once again by the wild, jungle quality of the foliage on the other side of the train tracks. You are drenched in sweat from the courts, your hands are gray with dirt. The air is smoky and filled with the rise and fall of cicada sounds. From all that, I get the idea to do a traveling shot for *Hemlock Forest*. I hold your shoulder with one hand and the camera high with the other.

EXPLOSIONS

After making *Jeanne Dielman*, Chantal told Delphine Seyrig, the star of her film, that she thought she no longer had the spark. You said that you thought you'd never again feel the euphoria of filmmaking. And Seyrig said to you: "You have to make, make, make. You still have the passion. You're just not an adolescent anymore."

You talked about manic episodes, explosions, which you'd put to use with bursts of work and creativity. You would "make, make, make," until you were spent, and then you'd remain dazed ("hébétée") for weeks afterward.

The woman making this film is writing on the subway, on the uptown 1 train in fact, but thinking of you four—Barney, Eric, Euripides, and Leo—in a house surrounded by woods and falling snow.

It was a brief encounter; she was meeting some of you for the first time.

You ate, you slept, you played ball, you got high, you stayed up all night.

The day before you left, she turned on the camera without asking. She's not adept; the picture goes in and out of focus.

She's fascinated by you, doesn't want to be a voyeur, knows she is doing just that, eavesdropping on you and your world. You are the opposite of low-hanging fruit.

She started filming, and you gave tacit permission. You were playful, funny. You performed. You were trusting. When she replays the footage, she's awed by your faces, your smiles, your jokes, your aliveness.

She feels alive when she's behind a camera, when she's shooting her own scenes, when she is making something.

2016

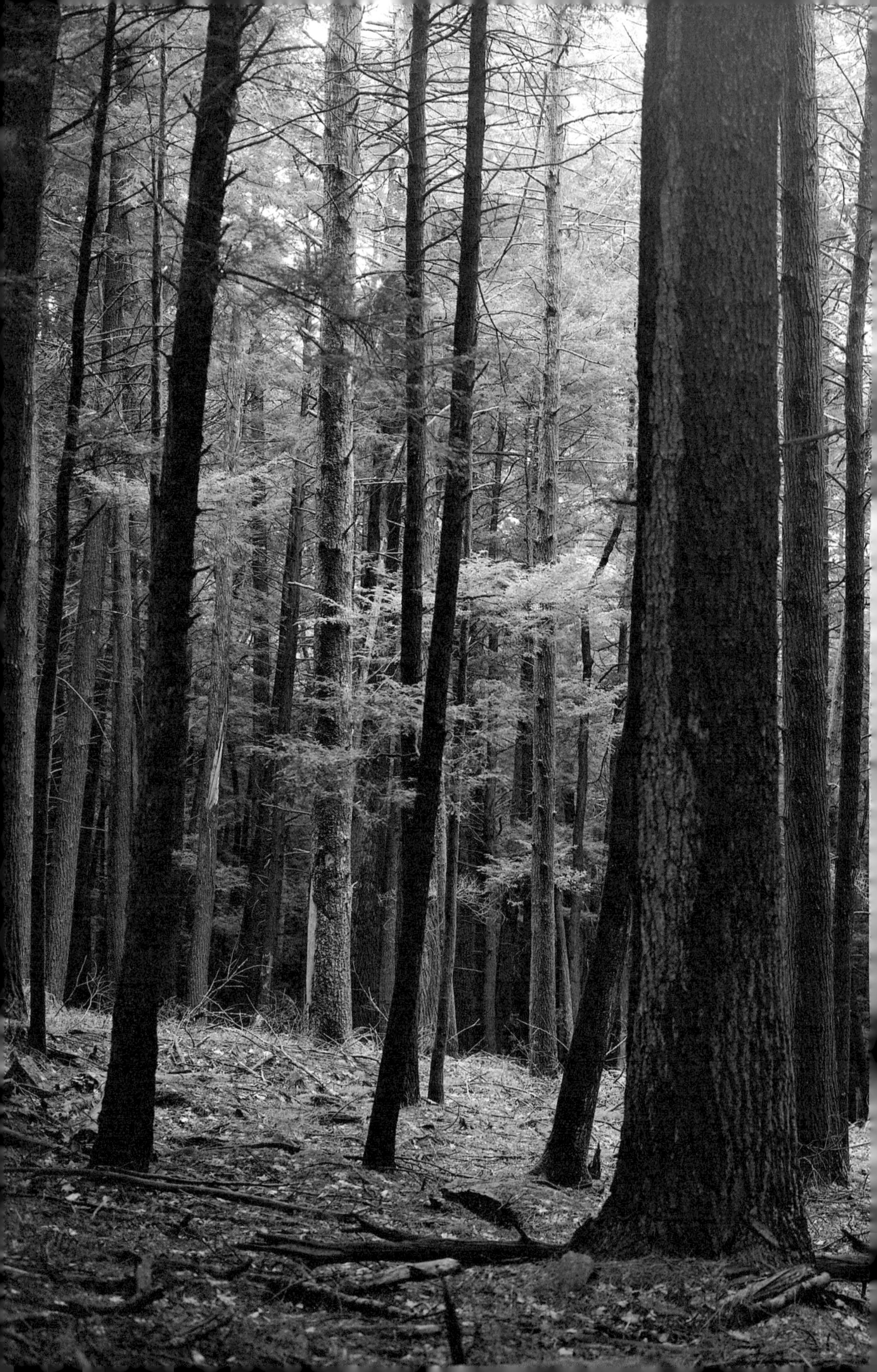

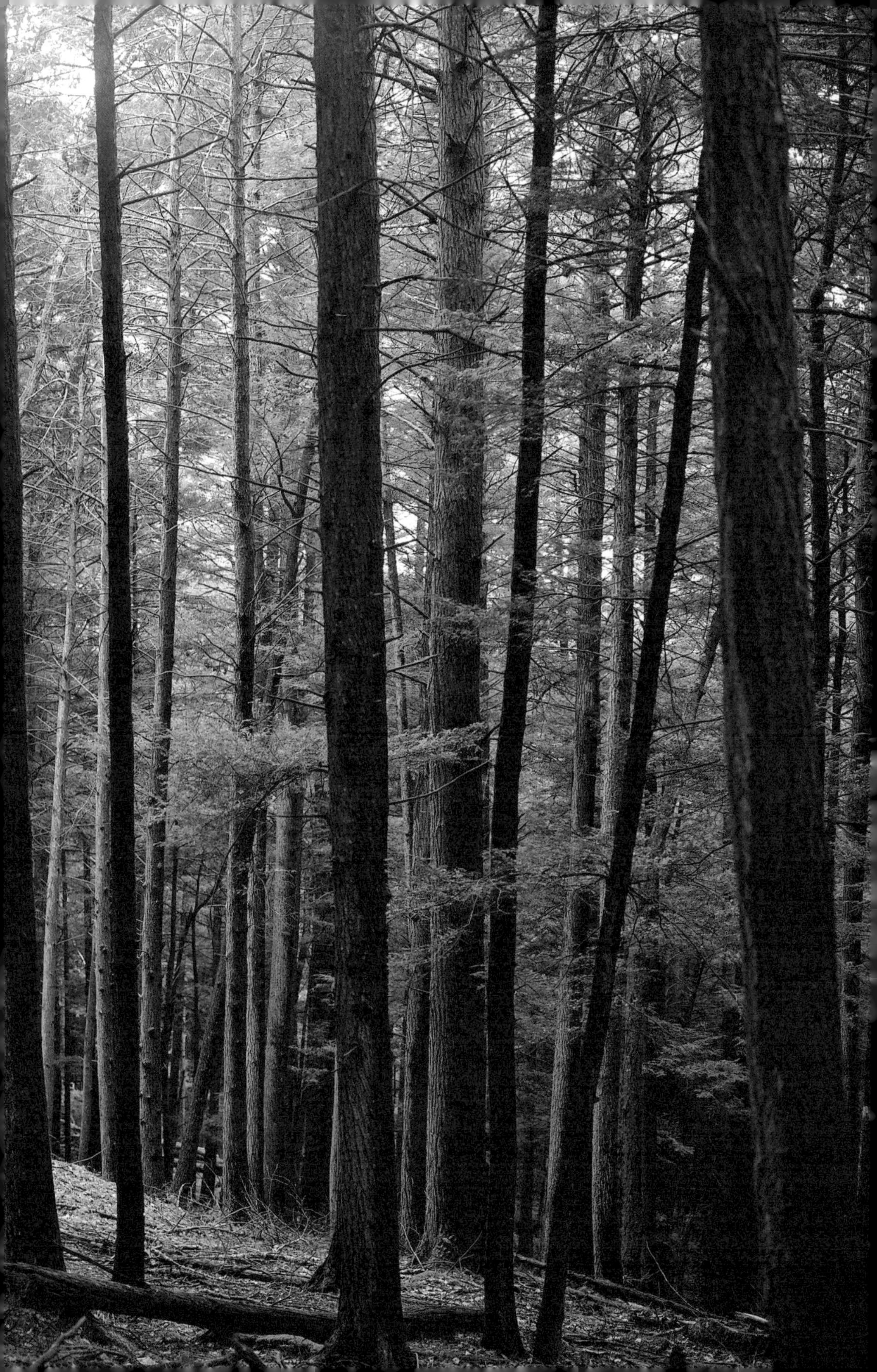

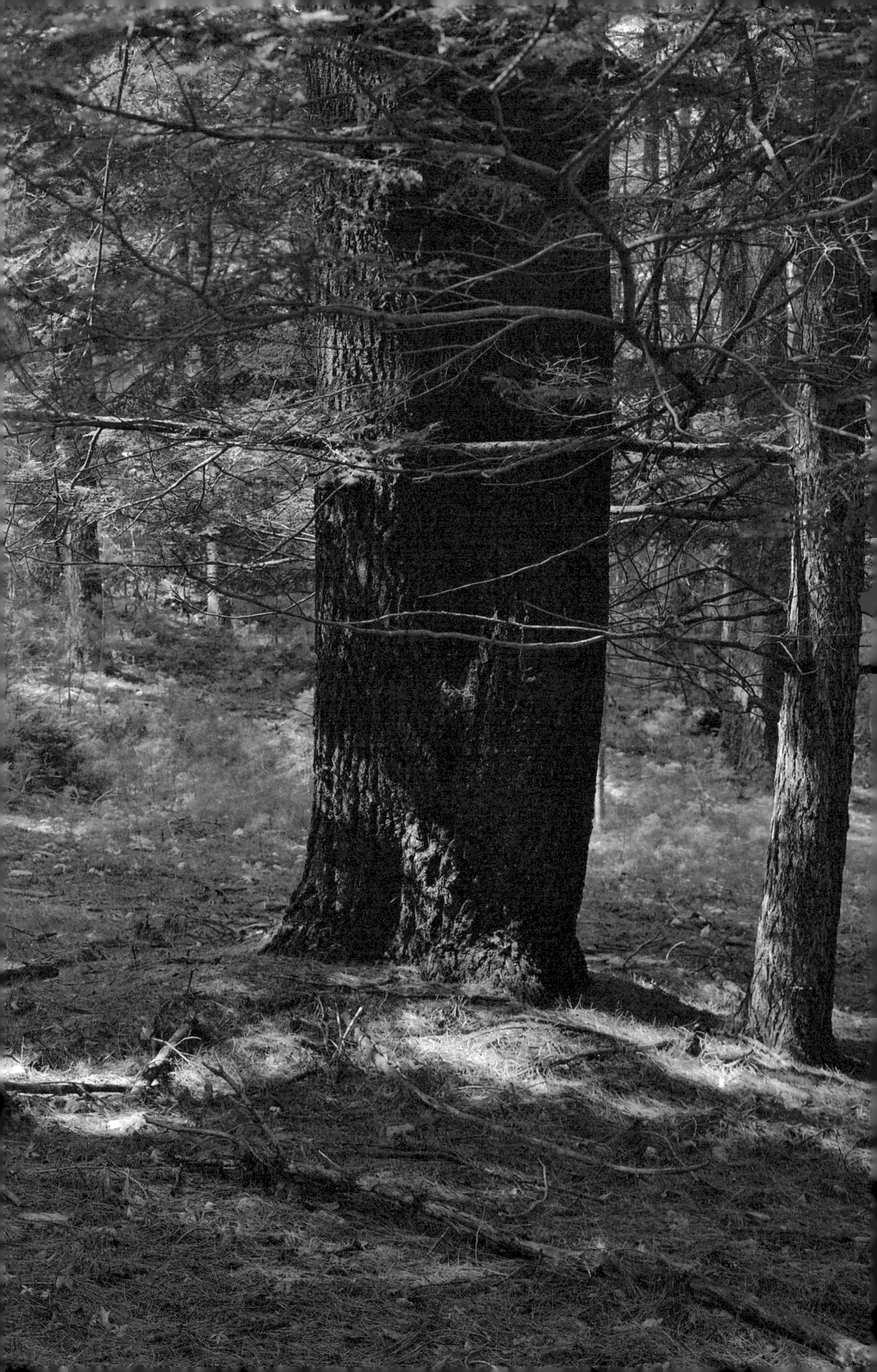